Grammar and Language Links

D1509330

DATE DUE

GAYLORD PRINTED IN U.S.A.

ELEMENTS OF
...erature
FIRST COURSE

WORKSHEETS
ANSWER KEY

Trinity Christian College
6601 W. College Dr.
Palos Heights, IL 60463

HOLT, RINEHART AND WINSTON
Harcourt Brace & Company
Austin • New York • Orlando • Atlanta • San Francisco • Boston • Dallas • Toronto • London

Staff Credits

Associate Director: Mescal Evler

Manager of Editorial Operations: Robert R. Hoyt

Project Editor: Katie Vignery

Component Editor: Scott Hall

Editorial Staff: *Associate Editor,* Kathryn Rogers; *Assistant Managing Editor,* Mandy Beard; *Copyediting Supervisor,* Michael Neibergall; *Senior Copyeditor,* Mary Malone; *Copyeditors,* Joel Bourgeois, Jon Hall, Jeffrey T. Holt, Jane Kominek, Susan Sandoval; *Editorial Coordinators,* Marie H. Price, Robert Littlefield, Mark Holland, Jill Chertudi, Marcus Johnson, Tracy DeMont; *Support Staff,* Pat Stover, Matthew Villalobos; *Word Processors,* Ruth Hooker, Margaret Sanchez, Kelly Keeley

Permissions: Tamara A. Blanken, Ann B. Farrar

Design: *Art Director, Book Design,* Richard Metzger; *Design Manager, Book & Media Design,* Joe Melomo

Prepress Production: Beth Prevelige, Simira Davis, Sergio Durante

Manufacturing Coordinator: Michael Roche

Copyright © by Holt, Rinehart and Winston

All rights reserved. No part of this publication may be reproduced or transmitted in any form or by any means, electronic or mechanical, including photocopy, recording, or any information storage and retrieval system, without permission in writing from the publisher.

Teachers using ELEMENTS OF LITERATURE may photocopy blackline masters in complete pages in sufficient quantities for classroom use only and not for resale.

Printed in the United States of America

ISBN 0-03-052357-5

7 8 9 10 022 06 05 04 03 02

Table of Contents

Copyright © by Holt, Rinehart and Winston. All rights reserved.

COLLECTION FOUR:
WE ROOKIES HAVE TO STICK TOGETHER

COLLECTION FIVE:
LIVING IN THE HEART

COLLECTION SIX:
THIS OLD EARTH

Copyright © by Holt, Rinehart and Winston. All rights reserved.

COLLECTION SEVEN:
OUR CLASSICAL HERITAGE

COLLECTION EIGHT:
900 CINDERELLAS: OUR WORLD HERITAGE IN FOLKLORE

Copyright © by Holt, Rinehart and Winston. All rights reserved.

To the Teacher

The copying masters in this *Grammar and Language Link Worksheets* booklet correspond to the Grammar Link and Language Link features, which follow the selections in the Pupil's Edition. These copying masters provide reinforcement, practice, and extension of the grammar and language skills presented in those features. Integrating language study with literature, worksheet examples and activities generally refer to the content of the selections.

The page number of the corresponding Grammar Link or Language Link feature in the Pupil's Edition is referenced on the copying masters for each selection.

Answer Key

The Answer Key provides answers to all objective questions in *Grammar and Language Link Worksheets,* as well as models or guidelines for responses to open-ended questions and activities.

Copyright © by Holt, Rinehart and Winston. All rights reserved.

NAME ______________________ CLASS ______________ DATE __________

LANGUAGE LINK

Rikki-tikki-tavi

Rudyard Kipling

Pupil's Edition page 21

Choosing Specific Verbs

Many words in the English language have similar meanings—some general, some more specific—but no two words mean exactly the same thing. In an action story, **specific verbs** add an element of interest and liveliness that may not exist with more common verbs. As you read the following passage, notice Rudyard Kipling's deliberate and effective use of vivid verbs, which have been italicized.

> "Then he *was battered* to and fro as a rat is shaken by a dog—to and fro on the floor, up and down, and round in great circles, but his eyes were red and he held on as the body *cartwhipped* over the floor, upsetting the tin dipper and the soap dish and the flesh brush, and *banged* against the tin side of the bath."

A verb is a word used to express action or a state of being.

	Action Verbs	Linking Verbs
General	run, talk	is, may be
Specific	trot, chatter	grow, taste

Carefully selected verbs create visual images in the mind of the reader. In the example above, for instance, the verbs *was battered, cartwhipped,* and *banged* create more interest than if the author had used *was thrown, rolled,* and *hit.*

EXERCISE A Recognizing Verbs

Underline five verbs in the following passage from "Rikki-tikki-tavi." Double-underline any you find particularly vivid.

"One day, a high summer flood washed him out of the burrow where he lived with his father and mother and carried him . . . down a roadside ditch. He found a little wisp of grass . . . there and clung to it till he lost his senses. When he revived, he was lying in the hot sun in the middle of a garden path, very draggled indeed, and a small boy was saying: 'Here's a dead mongoose. Let's have a funeral.' "

EXERCISE B Using Active Verbs

Each of the following verbs is from "Rikki-tikki-tavi." On the lines provided, use each verb in an original sentence.

1. swayed

____

____

Copyright © by Holt, Rinehart and Winston. All rights reserved.

2. coil

____

____

3. trot

____

____

4. sprang

____

____

5. creep

____

____

6. sobbed

____

____

7. shrieked

____

____

8. fluttered

____

____

9. crush

____

____

10. clucking

____

____

Copyright © by Holt, Rinehart and Winston. All rights reserved.

NAME ______________________ CLASS ______________ DATE ___________

GRAMMAR LINK

Song of the Trees

Mildred D. Taylor

Pupil's Edition page 44

Subject-Verb Agreement Is Unanimous!

She hears the song of the trees.
They hears the song of the trees.

How does changing just one word make a perfectly good sentence go wrong? As you probably noticed, the singular verb from the first sentence above *(hears)* does not agree when used with the plural subject in the second sentence *(They)*.

The first rule of subject-verb agreement is that **singular subjects take singular verbs and plural subjects take plural verbs.** Sometimes, though, it is hard to know if the subject is singular or plural. The following examples will help you determine when a subject is singular and when it is plural.

1. A prepositional phrase does not change the number of the subject.
The **color** of all the trees **has** changed. [*Color,* not *trees,* is the subject; it takes a singular verb.]
The **men** in the town **are** working. [*Men,* not *town,* is the subject; it takes a plural verb.]

2. The indefinite pronouns *anybody, anyone, each, either, everybody, everyone, neither, nobody, no one, one, somebody,* and *someone* take singular verbs.
Neither of the students **has** a book. [The singular pronoun *Neither,* not *students,* is the subject; it takes a singular verb.]
The indefinite pronouns *both, few, many,* and *several* take plural verbs.
Many in the room **remember** her. [The plural pronoun *Many,* not *room,* is the subject; it takes a plural verb.]
Some indefinite pronouns, such as *all, any, most,* and *none,* may be singular or plural, depending on whether the indefinite pronoun refers to one item or more than one item.
All of the dinner **was** removed from the table. [*All* refers to the singular noun *dinner,* so it takes a singular verb.]
All of the dishes **were** washed. [*All* refers to the plural noun *dishes,* so it takes a plural verb.]

3. Singular subjects joined by *and* take a plural verb.
The **book** and the **video were** available last year. [*Book* and *video* together take a plural verb.]
When subjects are joined by *or* or *nor,* the verb agrees with the closest subject.
Either David or the **girls are** expected to call. [The verb agrees with the plural subject *girls.*]
Neither the dogs nor the **cat has** fleas. [The verb agrees with the singular subject *cat.*]

4. Collective nouns take a singular verb when referring to the subject as a single group, or a plural verb when referring to the individual members of the group.
The **group waits** for **its** instructions. [The group as a unit waits.]
The **group wait** for **their** instructions. [The group of people wait.]

Copyright © by Holt, Rinehart and Winston. All rights reserved.

NAME ______________________ CLASS ______________ DATE ____________

EXERCISE A **Identifying Correct Subject-Verb Agreement**

In each sentence, if the italicized verb *does not* agree with the subject, circle the verb and write its correct form on the line provided. If the subject and verb agree, write **C** on the line.

_________ **1.** Big Ma and Cassie *shares* the same bedroom.

_________ **2.** All the trees—the pine, the black walnut, the hickory—*sing* to Cassie.

_________ **3.** Each of the trees *have* its own special personality.

_________ **4.** Little Man, the youngest of the children, *takes* pride in his appearance.

_________ **5.** Neither Mama nor Big Ma *wants* to sell the trees.

_________ **6.** Both of the women *feels* threatened by Mr. Andersen.

_________ **7.** All of the forest *sit* silently before them.

_________ **8.** Most of the trees *have* Xs marked on them.

_________ **9.** Cassie and her brothers *attacks* the lumbermen.

_________ **10.** The Logan family *hope* that Stacey and Mr. Logan will return in time.

EXERCISE B **Practicing Subject-Verb Agreement**

Circle the verb that agrees with the subject in each sentence.

A tree, and a tree, and another tree (*makes, make*) up my secret place. I come here when my duties or a brother (*drives, drive*) me crazy. (*Comes, Come*), Papa, soon, for the men and the truck (*has, have*) come to take my friends away. As each minute of every hour (*goes, go*) by, I grow more worried.

EXERCISE C **Completing Sentences Using the Correct Verb Form**

Complete each sentence using a verb form that agrees with the subject.

1. Mama, with the help of Cassie and her brothers, ______________________

____

2. Not one of David Logan's children ______________________

____

3. The Logans must decide whether the trees or the money ______________________

____

4. Neither Cassie nor her brothers ______________________

____

5. While David Logan holds the plunger, the group of men ______________________

____

Copyright © by Holt, Rinehart and Winston. All rights reserved.

NAME ______________________ CLASS ________________ DATE ____________

GRAMMAR LINK

The Smallest Dragonboy

Anne McCaffrey **Pupil's Edition page 63**

Keeping Verb Tenses Consistent

Keevan is small, but he has determination. When he was a baby, he probably walked before he crawled! He shows that attitude was very important.

"OK," you may be thinking, "I understand the first sentence. It's in the present tense, so the verbs are present tense verbs. I also understand the second sentence. It's in the past tense, so all the verbs are past tense verbs. So what is wrong with the third sentence?"

It's simple. The first two sentences use verb tense consistently. The verbs in the third sentence jump tenses.

Use present-tense verbs to talk about the present, and use past-tense verbs to talk about the past. Don't switch needlessly from one tense to another.

EXERCISE A Making the Tense Consistent

In each of the following sentences, circle the correct tense of the verb in parentheses. Use the tense that is consistent with the other verb(s) in the sentence.

1. He is twelve "turns" old when he (*attends, attended*) the Impression.
2. The Weyrwoman (*wants, wanted*) to know what Keevan remembered.
3. Keevan was marked as an underdog, just as the author's brother (*is, was*).
4. The author presents dragons in a way that (*makes, made*) us admire them.
5. The blue dragons (*are, were*) the ones that guarded the city.
6. Pern has an enemy that (*falls, fell*) from the sky.
7. Bronze dragons were large and (*fly, flew*) with the queen.
8. Keevan is the smallest dragonboy, but he (*has, had*) an honest heart.
9. Readers like to see what (*happens, happened*) to an underdog character.
10. Keevan thought he would burst with joy as he (*puts, put*) his arms around Heth.

EXERCISE B Telling the Story in the Present Tense

Choose the pair of verbs that best fits the meaning of each sentence. Then, fill in the blanks with the present tense of the verbs you choose. (Note: You may have to change the form of some verbs to make them agree with their subjects.)

work; hope	break; push	choose; hatch
touch; guard	struggle; overcome	

1. Keevan ________________ the egg that Beterli ________________.
2. The dragons ________________ as soon as they ________________.

Copyright © by Holt, Rinehart and Winston. All rights reserved.

3. Each dragonboy ________________ hard and ________________ to be chosen.

4. Beterli ________________ Keevan's leg when he ________________ him down.

5. Keevan ________________ with pain and ________________ it enough to walk a little.

EXERCISE C Talking About the Past

Using the past tense, fill in each blank with the verb in parentheses.

When Mrs. Sanchez (*ask*) ________________ her class what they (*think*) ________________ about "The Smallest Dragonboy," the students (*respond*) ________________ in various ways.

"It (*make*) ________________ me want to live on Pern!" exclaimed Adam.

"I (*do*) ________________ not like the idea of living in caves," commented Lida.

"I (*know*) ________________ Keevan would be chosen when Mende (*tell*) ________________ him what qualities the dragons (*look*) ________________ for in a boy."

EXERCISE D Proofreading

Proofread the following paragraph, and make all the verbs present tense. Circle each verb that is not in the present tense, and write the present tense verb form above it. There are five incorrect verb forms.

Keevan is eager to become a dragonboy, but when he is a candidate he was teased because of his small size. Beterli, an older boy, especially teases him about being small and thought Keevan shouldn't be allowed to be a candidate. That is why it becomes so important for Keevan to Impress a dragon—he wants to prove himself. There is talk one night at dinner that the younger candidates might have been disqualified because of the large ratio of dragonboys to eggs, so Keevan believes Beterli when he suggests that Keevan is disqualified from the Impression. In a scuffle afterward, Keevan falls and broke his leg. While he is in his bed recovering, the hatching begins. He decided to go to the hatching in spite of his broken leg. Once he gets there, however, he feels embarrassed and tries to hide. So no one is more surprised than Keevan himself when he Impresses the bronze dragon!

Copyright © by Holt, Rinehart and Winston. All rights reserved.

NAME ______________________ CLASS ______________ DATE ______________

GRAMMAR LINK

Three Skeleton Key

George G. Toudouze

Pupil's Edition page 79

Those Troublesome Verbs

"Quick, Le Gleo, *lie* Itchoua down and help me get this trapdoor shut before the rats push through!" I screamed.

"*Lay,*" responded Le Gleo.

"What?!" I cried.

"It's *lay,* not *lie,*" said Le Gleo. "*Lay* Itchoua down."

"Le Gleo! While you were giving me a grammar lesson, a dozen rats slipped in! Help me *sit* the door in place, now!"

In this dialogue that might have taken place between Le Gleo and the narrator of "Three Skeleton Key," you can almost see Le Gleo lifting his finger and opening his mouth to change *sit* to *set.* He would be right, of course. Here is a chart of a few more troublesome verbs.

sit	The verb *sit* means "to be seated" or "to rest." *Sit* never takes an object.	My backpack **sits** next to me. [no object]
set	The verb *set* means "to place" or "to put." *Set* usually takes an object.	I **set** my backpack next to me. [*Backpack* is the object.]
lie	The verb *lie* means "to recline" or "to remain in a certain position." *Lie* never takes an object.	The newspaper **lies** there every day. [no object]
lay	The verb *lay* means "to put (something) down" or "to place (something)." *Lay* usually takes an object.	You **lay** the newspaper there every day. [*Newspaper* is the object.]
rise	The verb *rise* means "to move upward" or "to go up." *Rise* never takes an object.	His hand **rises** quickly. [no object]
raise	The verb *raise* means "to lift (something) up." *Raise* usually takes an object.	The boy **raises** his hand quickly. [*Hand* is the object.]

If necessary, refer to the chart below while completing the following exercises.

Base Form	Present Participle	Past	Past Participle
sit	(is) sitting	sat	(have) sat
set	(is) setting	set	(have) set
lie	(is) lying	lay	(have) lain
lay	(is) laying	laid	(have) laid
rise	(is) rising	rose	(have) risen
raise	(is) raising	raised	(have) raised

Copyright © by Holt, Rinehart and Winston. All rights reserved.

NAME ______________________ CLASS ______________ DATE ____________

EXERCISE A Practice Using Those Troublesome Verbs

Choose the correct verb in parentheses to fill in each blank.

I (*lay/laid*) ______________ down the book I was reading. I had been (*sitting/setting*) ______________ in the lantern room for hours. It was still too early for the sun to (*rise/raise*) ______________, but the moonlight reflected brightly on the rocks outside the glass. I knew I should wake my partner and go (*lie/lay*) ______________ down, if only for an hour or two. And yet I (*sat/set*) ______________ there, my eyes closing, though I tried to stay awake.

A moment later, still struggling with sleep, I heard a strange sound. My eyes popped open! Three skeletal figures (*sat/set*) ______________ down one bony foot after another on the sea-drenched rocks. As they danced, they (*lay/laid*) ______________ their skinless fingers on their naked ribs. Clack, clack, clickity clack! Frightened, I (*rose/raised*) ______________ from my seat. "Oh, no! Not again," I thought. "Not here!"

"(*Lie/Lay*) ______________ down, Le Gleo," came a voice in the dark room. "You are dreaming." I (*rose/raised*) ______________ my eyes to the barred window of the asylum. Outside, the moon was full over the French countryside.

EXERCISE B Identifying the Correct Troublesome Verb

On the line next to each sentence, write **C** if the italicized verb is correct. If the verb is incorrect, write the correct form of the verb on the line before the sentence.

EXAMPLE: ___C___ Their skeletons *lie* hidden even to this day.

EXAMPLE: _raises_ He *rises* his hat from the hook and places it on his head.

__________ 1. Three Skeleton Key *lies* over twenty miles from the mainland.

__________ 2. One could *set* for hours watching the light dance over the ocean.

__________ 3. The men routinely *set* themselves to the task at hand.

__________ 4. It would have been necessary to *lay* down some ground rules.

__________ 5. They usually *rise* early to complete their work before the heat of the day.

__________ 6. They would often *rise* their eyes to the horizon in search of a ship.

__________ 7. The rescuers had *lain* meat on the barge to attract the rats.

__________ 8. As the rats fell into the sea, sharks *raised* their greedy jaws to catch them.

__________ 9. The door *sits* solidly on its hinges.

__________ 10. Their hopes began to *raise* when morning came.

Copyright © by Holt, Rinehart and Winston. All rights reserved.

NAME ______________________ CLASS ______________ DATE ____________

GRAMMAR LINK

A Day's Wait

Ernest Hemingway

Pupil's Edition page 87

Irregular Verbs Dare to Be Different

In the morning, she walked to the beach.

There she placed her towel on the sand.

She standed at the edge of the water.

Did you notice that although the verbs in the sentences above all follow the same pattern, the third one doesn't sound quite right? Most verbs in English follow the pattern of those in the first two sentences. These are called **regular verbs,** because they follow a regular pattern.

Present	Past	Past Participle
walk	walked	(have) walked
place	placed	(have) placed

There are some verbs, however, that break away from this pattern and have their own individual forms of the past and past participle tenses. These verbs are called **irregular verbs,** because they follow no regular pattern. Several common examples are listed in the Pupil's Edition; the following chart gives more examples.

Present	Past	Past Participle
bite	bit	(have) bitten *or* bit
bring	brought	(have) brought
eat	ate	(have) eaten
feel	felt	(have) felt
get	got	(have) got *or* gotten
go	went	(have) gone
know	knew	(have) known
lend	lent	(have) lent
make	made	(have) made
put	put	(have) put
ring	rang	(have) rung
shoot	shot	(have) shot
speak	spoke	(have) spoken
stand	stood	(have) stood
steal	stole	(have) stolen
take	took	(have) taken
throw	threw	(have) thrown
wake	woke *or* waked	(have) waked *or* woken
wear	wore	(have) worn

Copyright © by Holt, Rinehart and Winston. All rights reserved.

Unfortunately, there is no single rule to help us understand all the different ways irregular verbs change to form their past and past participle tenses. The only way to know irregular verb forms is to memorize them.

EXERCISE A Identifying Irregular Verbs

On the line next to each sentence, write **I** if the italicized verb is irregular. Write **R** if the verb is regular.

______ **1.** Mom and Dad *woke* to a sound during the night.

______ **2.** They heard the door *opening.*

______ **3.** Could they *lend* him an extra blanket?

______ **4.** He was *feeling* cold.

______ **5.** Mom *put* her hand against his cheek.

EXERCISE B Practicing the Past and Past Participle Forms of Irregular Verbs

Fill in the blank with the correct form of the verb in parentheses.

1. What time had he (*get*) ______________ up?

2. Papa (*steal*) ______________ into the room to see how he was.

3. Someone had (*ring*) ______________ for the doctor.

4. Schatz hadn't (*speak*) ______________ to anyone about his secret fear.

5. He got up and (*wear*) ______________ his regular clothes.

EXERCISE C Revising for Correct Use of Irregular Verbs

In the paragraph below, circle the incorrect irregular verb forms. Write the correct form of each verb above it. Make sure you write the verb in the correct tense. As an example, the first incorrect irregular verb has been identified and corrected. Find ten more.

eaten

Having (ate) the warm food maked Schatz feel a little better. He feeled more alive as soon as he bited into the cooked quail. Papa knowed that Schatz might be lonely if he taked a walk that afternoon, but he goed anyway. Papa standed near the lake and throwed a stick for the dog. On the way home, he shooted two birds for dinner. Schatz's face brightened when Papa bringed him the wonderful meal.

Copyright © by Holt, Rinehart and Winston. All rights reserved.

NAME ______________________ CLASS ______________ DATE ____________

LANGUAGE LINK

from Homesick

Jean Fritz

Pupil's Edition page 120

Style: Shades of Meaning—Denotations and Connotations

In "Homesick," Jean Fritz uses the word *old-fashioned* to describe the Chinese practice of binding a little girl's feet. What impression does the word *old-fashioned* give you?

What if Jean had said that she thought the practice of binding feet was *traditional*? Would this give you a different impression?

Old-fashioned and *traditional* have the same basic meaning, or **denotation,** but *traditional* has a more positive connotation for some people. A **connotation** is the emotional association that a word has. *Old-fashioned* implies that Jean thinks binding feet is out-of-date and somewhat silly, while *traditional* implies that it is a custom that should be respected.

Can you see the differences between the words in the following chart?

Negative Connotation	Positive Connotation
immature	youthful
frail	delicate
old	antique

When you write, it's important to think about the connotations of the words that you use. Using a word without knowing its connotation could send the wrong message!

EXERCISE A **Recognizing Positive and Negative Connotations**

The words in each of the following pairs have similar denotations, or definitions, but they have different connotations. Underline the word from each pair that has a negative connotation. Then, on the line below each pair of words, explain how the two words are different.

EXAMPLE: <u>yank</u>, pull

A yank is a quick pull that hurts.

1. narrow, cramped

____

2. imposing, grand

____

3. grunted, murmured

____

4. dangled, drooped

____

Copyright © by Holt, Rinehart and Winston. All rights reserved.

5. stubborn, determined

____

6. timid, careful

____

7. proud, arrogant

____

8. puzzled, distressed

____

EXERCISE B Changing the Connotation of a Sentence

In the space provided, replace the word in italics with a word that has the same meaning but a more positive connotation. Be careful not to change the meaning of the sentence. You may need to use a thesaurus.

EXAMPLE: ____tucked____ Lin Nai-Nai's tiny feet were *stuffed* into cloth shoes.

____________ 1. As the class sang, Miss Williams kept time by *striking* the ruler against a shelf.

____________ 2. "Why aren't you singing the anthem?" Miss Williams *snapped.*

____________ 3. Jean *slouched* against the stone wall and watched the clouds.

____________ 4. Ian Forbes *grabbed* Jean's arm.

____________ 5. The little boy *glared* at Jean.

EXERCISE C Using Negative and Positive Connotations

Write a sentence describing the following topics from the selection, giving each a positive or negative connotation, as indicated in brackets.

1. the Yangtze River [positive]

____

2. the British school [positive]

____

3. Ian Forbes [positive]

____

4. the Bund [negative]

____

5. the Chinese junk [negative]

____

Copyright © by Holt, Rinehart and Winston. All rights reserved.

GRAMMAR LINK

from Barrio Boy

Ernesto Galarza

Pupil's Edition page 133

Making the Most of Comparing Adjectives and Adverbs

"This is the most bestest story we've read this year," says Kim.
"That's not right!" responds Kim's friend.
"What do you mean? I liked this story!" replies Kim.
"No, I mean that you can't say *most bestest,*" corrects Kim's friend. "You never use *most* with *bestest*. But I do agree about the story. I liked it the bestest, too."

Who's right? Kim's friend is right about one thing, at least; *more* and *most* are not used with comparisons that end with *-er* or *-est.* However, the comparative and superlative forms of *good—better* and *best—*are irregular. They don't use *more* and *most* or *-er* and *-est,* so *bestest* is also incorrect. Neither Kim nor Kim's friend has it quite right.

There are three degrees of comparison for modifiers: the positive, the comparative, and the superlative.

- The positive degree is used when only one thing is being described.
- The comparative degree is used when two things are being compared.
- The superlative degree is used when three or more things are being compared.

Short modifiers (most one-syllable and some two-syllable words) form the comparative and superlative degrees by adding *-er* and *-est.*

Positive	Comparative	Superlative
big	bigger	biggest
little	littler	littlest

Longer modifiers (many two-syllable words and most with three or more syllables) form the comparative degree by using *more* and the superlative by using *most.*

Positive	Comparative	Superlative
clearly	more clearly	most clearly
fantastic	more fantastic	most fantastic

Of course, there are a few irregular forms that simply must be memorized.

Positive	Comparative	Superlative
bad	worse	worst
far	farther	farthest
good	better	best
well	better	best
many	more	most
much	more	most

Copyright © by Holt, Rinehart and Winston. All rights reserved.

NAME ______________________ CLASS ______________ DATE ____________

EXERCISE A Practicing Making Comparisons

Each of the following sentences contains an italicized modifier. Fill in the blank with the correct comparative or superlative form of the modifier.

EXAMPLE: The principal is *encouraging,* but the teacher is more encouraging.

1. It is *interesting* to learn about your culture, but comparing your culture to another one is even ______________.
2. Miss Ryan's class has *many* students, but Mrs. Johnson's class has ______________.
3. Ernesto is *nervous* when he enters the school, but he is ______________ when his mother leaves him there.
4. Ernesto and Matti wrestle *well,* but Manuel wrestles the ______________.
5. Ernesto has to walk *far* to get to school, but many students walk ______________.
6. Adjusting to a new culture can be *difficult,* but it is even ______________ if you are expected to give up your own customs and traditions.
7. Ernesto is a *good* speller, but he is a ______________ reader.
8. Mr. Galarza is an *understanding* teacher. He is probably the ______________ teacher at school.
9. The children don't have *much* homework in elementary school. They will have ______________ in high school.
10. Reading about real-life experiences is *educational,* but living them is ______________.

EXERCISE B Proofreading for Incorrect Modifiers

Each of the sentences in the following paragraph contains an error in the use of a modifier. Cross out each incorrect modifier and write the correct form above it.

EXAMPLE: Ernesto liked Matti, but he liked Manuel the ~~best~~. better

When Ernesto first met Miss Ryan, he thought she was the most tallest woman he had ever seen. Although he was frightened by her at first, he soon decided that she was more nicer than any other teacher at the school. He felt as if she were proudest of him than she was of anyone else. Miss Ryan was happy when any student read a new sentence, but Ernesto thought that she was happier when he read his sentence. While he always worked hard at school, he worked even hardest when she was helping him.

Copyright © by Holt, Rinehart and Winston. All rights reserved.

NAME ______________________ CLASS ______________ DATE ___________

LANGUAGE LINK

Fish Cheeks

Amy Tan **Pupil's Edition page 143**

Style: Using Precise Adjectives

"I'm not sure which one of these books to read next," Lawrence says.

"I just finished the one over there," responds Elizabeth. "It's a good one."

"The book I read was exciting and suspenseful," offers Sylvia. "I just couldn't put it down."

Based upon the recommendations given by Elizabeth and Sylvia, which book do you think Lawrence will choose? Elizabeth says her book is good, but good in what way? Sylvia tells more precisely what she likes about her book. The adjective *good* is vague, while *exciting* and *suspenseful* are more specific. Watch for more **precise adjectives** as we see which of the girls' suggestions Lawrence finds more intriguing.

"Wow! It was exciting and suspenseful? Which book was it, Sylvia?" asks Lawrence.

"It's that little orange one in the middle of the bottom shelf," she answers.

"Hey! That's the same story I read," says Elizabeth. "I told you it was good."

An adjective is a word used to modify a noun or a pronoun by telling *what kind, which one,* or *how many.* Using precise, descriptive adjectives makes conversation and writing more interesting and informative.

EXERCISE A Identifying Descriptive Adjectives

Underline the descriptive adjectives in the following sentences.

EXAMPLE: I pulled the vein, stringy and black, out of the juicy, pink shrimp.

1. Amy was a young teenager, sensitive and impressionable.
2. Being the only Chinese girl in the class made Amy uncomfortable.
3. She longed for a narrow American nose.
4. Slimy, pale, raw seafood littered the counter.
5. She tried without success to ignore her unsophisticated relatives.
6. The pudding-soft cheek below the flattened, cooked eye was her favorite part.
7. Robert tried to hide his reddened face by looking down.
8. The minister did all he could to be polite and courteous.
9. The beige tweed miniskirt was just the right style.
10. Now older and wiser, Amy has a better understanding of herself and her mother.

Copyright © by Holt, Rinehart and Winston. All rights reserved.

NAME ______________________ CLASS ______________ DATE ____________

EXERCISE B Adding Precise Adjectives

On the lines below each sentence, write one or more adjectives to fill in the blank space in the sentence. On the first line, write adjectives that will give the sentence a positive meaning, and on the second line, write adjectives that will give the sentence a negative meaning.

EXAMPLE: The ________ blush of her cheek let him know what she thought of him.

POSITIVE: charming; rosy; dainty

NEGATIVE: angry; embarrassed

1. Mother set the ______ meal on the table.

   POSITIVE: ______________________________

   NEGATIVE: ______________________________

2. My ______ relatives greeted the guests.

   POSITIVE: ______________________________

   NEGATIVE: ______________________________

3. They came into our ______ living room.

   POSITIVE: ______________________________

   NEGATIVE: ______________________________

4. My father spoke to the ______ man.

   POSITIVE: ______________________________

   NEGATIVE: ______________________________

5. I wore my ______ shirt to the dinner.

   POSITIVE: ______________________________

   NEGATIVE: ______________________________

6. The ______ evening would soon be over!

   POSITIVE: ______________________________

   NEGATIVE: ______________________________

7. She remembered the ______ years of her youth.

   POSITIVE: ______________________________

   NEGATIVE: ______________________________

Copyright © by Holt, Rinehart and Winston. All rights reserved.

NAME ____________________ CLASS ______________ DATE __________

GRAMMAR LINK

Names/Nombres

Julia Alvarez — **Pupil's Edition page 151**

Don't Leave Your Modifiers Dangling

Having no fear of falling, learning to skate was easy.

What's wrong with the sentence above? Do you understand the writer's meaning? Probably, but something very important is missing from the sentence. Who is it that has no fear of falling?

The subject of the sentence is *learning to skate;* but it is neither *learning* nor *skating* that has no fear of falling. The phrase *having no fear of falling* does not modify any of the words in the sentence. The noun (or pronoun) modified by the opening phrase is missing from the sentence. When a modifier appears in a sentence without the word to which it refers, it is called a **dangling modifier.** Can you think of a way to correct the dangling modifier in the example at the top of the page? Write your solution here:

____

Two possible methods for correcting the dangling modifier in the example above are printed upside down at the bottom of the page.

See if you can spot the dangling modifiers in the following exercises.

EXERCISE A Identifying Dangling Modifiers

Each of the following sentences contains a modifying phrase. If the italicized phrase is a dangling modifier, write **DM** on the line provided. If the phrase is *not* a dangling modifier (that is, the sentence contains the noun or pronoun modified by the phrase), underline the modified word or phrase.

______ 1. *Yelling "Little girl!"* I was caught playing on the elevators.

______ 2. *Referring to Shakespeare as my friend,* my mother quoted, "A rose by any other name would smell as sweet."

______ 3. *Beginning to see myself as popular,* my friends called me Jules and Hey Jude.

______ 4. *Not realizing the difference,* Mao-ree-shee-ah became Moor-ee-sha.

______ 5. *With an old TV commercial in mind,* Ana was called Anita Banana.

______ 6. *Suddenly interested in ethnicity,* people in the 1960s began trying to pronounce foreign names correctly.

______ 7. *Wondering if it would ever end,* friends listened in amazement to my entire name.

Copyright © by Holt, Rinehart and Winston. All rights reserved.

Since Paula had no fear of falling, learning to skate was easy.
Having no fear of falling, I found it easy to learn to skate.

______ **8.** *Feeling especially Dominican,* the graduation ceremony was packed with my relatives.

______ **9.** *Reaping the benefits of a large family,* I received one gift after another at my graduation party.

______ **10.** *Expecting to become a writer,* the typewriter was the most exciting gift of all.

EXERCISE B Correcting Dangling Modifiers

Each of the following sentences contains a dangling modifier. Correct each sentence by rewriting it to include a noun or pronoun modified by the italicized phrase. It will be necessary to change, rearrange, add, or delete words to correct the sentences.

EXAMPLE: *Introducing my relatives to my friends*, my friends' faces showed some surprise.

As I introduced my relatives to my friends, my friends' faces showed some surprise.

or

Introducing my relatives to my friends, I saw some surprise in my friends' faces.

1. *Trying hard to say it the way Julia did,* the word still sounded different coming out of me.

____

____

2. *Blushing at all the attention,* the other women wanted to know the baby's name.

____

____

3. *Feeling embarrassed by his own accent,* his name became more and more Americanized.

____

____

4. Questions about her native culture no longer bothered her, *finding her classmates interested in what she told them.*

____

____

5. *Convinced that her friends really liked her,* the nicknames they gave her were a sign of their affection.

____

____

____

Copyright © by Holt, Rinehart and Winston. All rights reserved.

NAME ______________________ CLASS ______________ DATE ____________

GRAMMAR LINK

The Naming of Names

Ray Bradbury

Pupil's Edition page 167

All Modifiers! Places, Please!

Piano for sale by woman upstairs with carved legs.

Do you wonder how many people answered this advertisement just to see the woman's carved legs? Of course, it wasn't the woman who had carved legs, but the piano. The confusion in the meaning of the sentence is due to a **misplaced modifier.**

The words *with carved legs* are a **prepositional phrase** describing (or modifying) the word *piano*. Since phrases that work as modifiers should always be placed as close as possible to the words they modify, the advertisement should have read

Piano *with carved legs* for sale by woman upstairs.

Participial phrases and **adjective clauses** may also be used as noun modifiers. They, too, can become misplaced modifiers if they are not placed close to the words they modify.

Using a Participial Phrase

MISPLACED: Tim put the dog out for the night having brushed his teeth.
CLEAR: Having brushed his teeth, Tim put the dog out for the night.

Using an Adjective Clause

MISPLACED: She showed the photo to the class that she had found.
CLEAR: She showed the photo that she had found to the class.

EXERCISE A Identifying Misplaced Modifiers

In each of the following sentences, underline the modifying clause or phrase. If the clause or phrase is misplaced, write an **M** on the line before the sentence.

EXAMPLE: __M__ He noticed the grass was purple which had been green.

______ **1.** The newcomers who arrived from Earth headed for the settlement.

______ **2.** Not understanding Harry's fear, Cora tried to calm him.

______ **3.** The peach tree grew a new type of blossom that they brought with them.

______ **4.** Glowing green in the east, Harry noticed the star.

______ **5.** They wondered if the Martians who had lived there first were still in the hills.

______ **6.** The wind had an effect on the Earth people that blew into the valley.

______ **7.** Made of blue marble, they moved into the Martian ruins.

______ **8.** Bathed with mist, the lieutenant gazed at the blue hills.

Copyright © by Holt, Rinehart and Winston. All rights reserved.

NAME ______________________ CLASS ______________ DATE ______________

EXERCISE B Correct Placement of Modifiers

Rewrite each of the following sentences, adding the modifying phrase given in parentheses. Be careful to place each phrase near the word or words it modifies.

EXAMPLE: Harry thought the blossoms looked different. (from the peach tree)
Harry thought the blossoms from the peach tree looked different.

1. Harry began to panic. (with no way to get home) ______________________

2. One of the first signs of change was seen in the eyes. (of the people) ______________________

3. The blue marble was as cool as ice. (in the villa) ______________________

4. Everyone moved to the hills during the summer. (in the settlement) ______________________

5. The men expected the settlers to be excited to see them. (from the rocket) ______________________

EXERCISE C Adding Modifiers to Sentences

Add a phrase or clause to modify the italicized word or phrase.

EXAMPLE: *Harry* found it difficult to build a rocket.
Working alone, Harry found it difficult to build a rocket.

1. Harry would not eat the *food.* ______________________

2. *The other men* sat and watched Harry work. ______________________

3. *The earth houses* flaked and peeled in the Martian summer. ______________________

4. They explored the *marble villas.* ______________________

5. Even *Harry* grew to like life on Mars. ______________________

Copyright © by Holt, Rinehart and Winston. All rights reserved.

NAME ______________________ CLASS ______________ DATE ____________

GRAMMAR LINK

After Twenty Years

O. Henry

Pupil's Edition page 201

End All End-Mark Errors

> One man came a thousand miles to keep a twenty-year-old appointment the other man came only a few steps was either of them happy with the way the evening turned out

Can you figure out where one thought ends and the next begins in the paragraph above? You probably can, but only after reading the lines a few times. This herd of words lacks end marks telling the reader where one thought ends and another begins. Notice how much easier it is to read the same group of words when end marks are added.

> One man came a thousand miles to keep a twenty-year-old appointment. The other man came only a few steps. Was either of them happy with the way the evening turned out?

End marks are the punctuation marks used at the ends of sentences. There are only three choices of end marks: periods, question marks, and exclamation points.

Use a period at the end of a statement.

I haven't seen my friend for twenty years**.**

Use a question mark at the end of a question.

Have you heard from him recently**?**

Use an exclamation point at the end of an exclamation.

I haven't heard a word for eighteen years**!**

Use either a period or an exclamation point at the end of a request or a command.

Please meet me at the restaurant**.** (request)

Don't be late**!** (command)

NOTE: Remember that any sentence, whether it is a statement, a question, an exclamation, or a command, must include a subject and a verb and express a complete thought.

EXERCISE A Adding End Marks to Sentences

Rewrite each of the following sentences on the lines provided. Insert end marks and capital letters where they are needed.

EXAMPLE: Jimmy seems at home on his beat he seems content with his life

Jimmy seems at home on his beat. He seems content with his life.

1. Do you have the impression that Jimmy likes his job do you think he is envious of Bob's money

____

____

Copyright © by Holt, Rinehart and Winston. All rights reserved.

2. What do you think Jimmy was thinking as he walked away from Bob that night must have been a disappointment for him

____

____

3. How do you think Bob feels about Jimmy he must be surprised that Jimmy turned him in

____

____

4. Bob probably wishes he had missed his appointment with Jimmy do you think Jimmy is glad he kept the date, or not

____

____

5. What a shock Jimmy and Bob ended up on opposite sides of the law

____

____

EXERCISE B **Proofreading for End Marks**

Proofread the following paragraphs. Add end marks (and capitalization) where they are needed. Change or delete end marks if they are incorrect. The first error has been corrected for you as an example.

Can you imagine how Bob must have felt when he read Jimmy's note? He must have felt as if he had been betrayed by his old friend the story tells us that Bob's hand began to shake when he read the note. Why did his hand shake. Was he angry. Maybe he was embarrassed that Jimmy knew the truth about him after all, he had led a life of crime while Jimmy had remained honest.

And what about Jimmy. Was he happy that a criminal was in jail was he sad that his old friend had ruined his life how do you think Jimmy felt when Bob suggested that Jimmy had always been a bit dull! He probably didn't get too angry at Bob Jimmy may not have made a fortune, but at least he had led an honest life. Bob bragged that he had made his fortune by his wits, but his "dull" friend had outwitted him this night?

Copyright © by Holt, Rinehart and Winston. All rights reserved.

NAME ______________________ CLASS ______________ DATE __________

GRAMMAR LINK

A Mason-Dixon Memory

Clifton Davis

Pupil's Edition page 215

Commas Make Sense of a Series

Clifton's class was planning to visit the Lincoln Memorial Arlington National Cemetery and Glen Echo Amusement Park.

Where does the name of one place stop and another begin? Without commas in the sentence it's hard to tell that the three places the class planned to visit were the Lincoln Memorial, Arlington National Cemetery, and Glen Echo Amusement Park. Use commas to separate words, phrases, or clauses in a series.

Words in a Series
The class visited monuments, museums, and other historical sites. **(nouns)**
Clifton was sad, angry, and confused. **(adjectives)**
Frank stopped, stared, and then smiled at Clifton. **(verbs)**

Phrases in a Series
Flopping on the bed, crying, and refusing to talk, Clifton had Frank worried. **(participial phrases)**

Clauses in a Series
Frank didn't know where Clifton went, what was wrong, or how to talk to him. **(subordinate clauses)**
Clifton's friends supported him, the chaperone got baseball tickets, and everyone had a good time. **(short independent clauses)**

- Only short independent clauses in a series may be separated by commas. Longer independent clauses in a series are separated by semicolons.

  Clifton and his friends all had a good time at the baseball game; they were glad that the Senators won the game.

- Do not place a comma between an adjective and a noun immediately following it.

  INCORRECT: The trip to the nation's capital was a fun, educational, vacation.

  CORRECT: The trip to the nation's capital was a fun, educational vacation.

- If the last adjective in a series is closely connected to the meaning of the noun, do not use a comma before that adjective.

  INCORRECT: It was fun to stay in a new, high-rise hotel.

  CORRECT: It was fun to stay in a new high-rise hotel.

To decide whether you need a comma, add the word *and* between the adjectives. If the sentence sounds strange, then don't use the comma. (*New and high-rise hotel* sounds strange, so don't use a comma.)

Copyright © by Holt, Rinehart and Winston. All rights reserved.

NAME ______________________ CLASS ______________ DATE ____________

EXERCISE A Placing Commas in a Series

In the following sentences, put commas where they are needed to separate words, phrases, or clauses in a series. If no commas are needed, put a ✓ in front of the sentence.

EXAMPLE: Clifton's class enjoyed a visit to the Lincoln Memorial, a Potomac River cruise, and a baseball game.

1. The story portrays Dondré as a soft-spoken friendly likable person.
2. Dondré approached the microphone and began to speak.
3. The seniors listened to their coach looked at one another and walked off the golf course.
4. Dondré ended his story tears came to his eyes and the audience applauded.
5. Clifton Davis is a writer songwriter singer and actor.
6. Clifton was impressed by the huge marble statue of Lincoln.
7. He noticed Lincoln's tired unsmiling face.
8. The white marble statue was bathed in warm yellow light.
9. Clifton was young ambitious and outgoing.
10. Dondré's friends were loving courageous and fair-minded.

EXERCISE B Proofreading for Correct Use of Commas in a Series

In the following paragraph, add commas where they are needed to separate words, phrases, or clauses that appear in a series. Circle commas that are incorrectly used. You should find ten errors. The first error has been corrected for you.

Both Dondré and Clifton feel the pain, anger and frustration of being targets of discrimination. However, both have caring honorable friends who stand by them. Also, both young African American, men put racism behind them go on with their lives and achieve success. Dondré speaks as the guest of honor at a banquet expresses his gratitude to his teammates and receives a standing ovation. Clifton's loyal boyhood friends make him proud and grateful. His confidence ambition and success may be, in part, a gift from them.

Copyright © by Holt, Rinehart and Winston. All rights reserved.

NAME ______________________ CLASS ______________ DATE ____________

GRAMMAR LINK

The No-Guitar Blues

Gary Soto

Pupil's Edition page 225

Put That Splice on Ice

Fausto wanted a guitar, he didn't have enough money to buy one.

Is there anything wrong with this sentence? If you said yes, you're right. If you said that it's a run-on, you're right again. A run-on sentence occurs when two sentences are incorrectly punctuated as one. The words above actually form two complete sentences that should not be connected with a comma. A run-on that connects two complete sentences with a comma is called a **comma splice.** You can correct a comma splice by breaking the sentence into two simple sentences.

Fausto wanted a guitar**. He** didn't have enough money to buy one.

You can also correct a comma splice by joining the two independent clauses with a conjunction—such as *and, but, for, or, nor, so,* or *yet*—and placing a comma before the conjunction.

Fausto wanted a guitar**, but** he didn't have enough money to buy one.

Be careful not to mistake a simple sentence with a compound verb for a run-on sentence. A simple sentence has only one independent clause.

Fausto walked up to the house and knocked on the door. [simple sentence with compound verb]

Fausto walked up to the house, and he knocked on the door. [compound sentence]

EXERCISE A Identifying Comma Splices

Write an **I** (for incorrect) on the line before each sentence that contains a comma splice. If the sentence is correct, write **C.**

______ **1.** He suddenly had a new direction for his life, he would become a rock star!

______ **2.** His mother listened to his request, could he have a guitar for Christmas?

______ **3.** His mother told him that they didn't have much money, but she would think about buying him a guitar.

______ **4.** A smart kid like Fausto ought to be able to think of a solution, for instance, he could earn the money to buy the guitar.

______ **5.** Fausto found that it takes more than the willingness to work, you must get hired!

EXERCISE B Correcting Comma Splices

Correct each sentence below that has a comma splice. Your corrected version may be one sentence or two. If the sentence is already punctuated correctly, write **C** on the line provided.

1. Fausto knows his family is not rich, that doesn't stop him from asking for a guitar.

____

____

Copyright © by Holt, Rinehart and Winston. All rights reserved.

NAME ______________________ CLASS ______________ DATE ____________

2. Programs like *American Bandstand* inspire as well as entertain, many viewers imitate dancers and musicians they see on TV.

____

____

3. You shouldn't expect others to solve your problems for you, find a way to do it for yourself.

____

____

4. Fausto's mother prepares many traditional foods, such as tortillas, chorizo con huevos, and papas.

____

____

5. After looking for work for three hours, Fausto is discouraged, he does not go home.

____

____

6. The dog presents a chance to make some money, Fausto looks for the dog's home.

____

____

7. Fausto doesn't like taking the money from Roger's kind owners, but how would he feel if they had not been so nice?

____

____

8. The collection basket comes to Fausto, he puts his twenty into the basket.

____

____

9. Does Fausto really fool Roger's owners, after all, they seem anxious to help him.

____

____

10. Fausto and his grandfather may not like the same music, Grandpa enjoys teaching him to play the guitarron.

____

____

Copyright © by Holt, Rinehart and Winston. All rights reserved.

NAME ______________________ CLASS ______________ DATE ____________

GRAMMAR LINK

Bargain

A. B. Guthrie **Pupil's Edition page 243**

End the Apostrophe Glut

"Is this book Jana's?"

"I'm not sure, but I think it's probably her's."

One of the apostrophes used above is incorrect. Do you know which one it is?

Jana's is a possessive noun and requires an apostrophe. *I'm* and *it's* are contractions, and they also require apostrophes. That leaves *her's* as the word that incorrectly uses an apostrophe. To find out why, keep reading!

There are three reasons to use an apostrophe:

(1) to form the possessive case of nouns and some pronouns;
(2) to indicate in a contraction where letters have been left out; and
(3) to form some plurals.

1. The possessive case of a noun shows ownership or relationship.

- To form the possessive of a singular noun, add *'s*.

  The horse**'s** reins are tied to the post.

- To form the possessive of a plural noun ending in *s*, add an apostrophe.

  The citizens**'** decision was to talk to the sheriff.

- To form the possessive of a plural noun not ending in *s*, add *'s*.

  The men**'s** activities made them look suspicious.

2. A contraction is a shortened form of a word, a figure, or a group of words. To form a contraction, use an apostrophe to show where letters have been left out.

Common Contractions			
cannot →	can't	I would →	I'd
does not →	doesn't	there is →	there's
I am →	I'm	they will →	they'll

Do not confuse contractions with the possessive form of pronouns such as *its, whose,* and *theirs*.

Contractions:	*It's* time to go.	[*It is* time to go.]
	Who's at the store?	[*Who is* at the store?]
	There's a problem.	[*There is* a problem.]
Possessives:	What is *its* title?	[What is *the book's* title?]
	Whose bill is it?	[*To whom* does the bill belong?]
	This bill is *theirs.*	[This bill belongs *to them.*]

Copyright © by Holt, Rinehart and Winston. All rights reserved.

NAME ______________________ CLASS ______________ DATE ______________

3. Use an apostrophe and an *s* to form the plurals of letters, numerals, and symbols, and of words referred to as words.

   The word *saddle* has two *d*'s, not one.

EXERCISE A **Rewriting Sentences with Singular and Plural Possessives**

Rewrite each of the following sentences. Revise the italicized phrase to use the possessive case. Be sure to insert apostrophes in the right places.

EXAMPLE: *The job that Al had* was only part time. Al's job was only part time.

1. Al worked in *a store owned by Mr. Baumer.* ______________________

____

2. There were two horses tied to *the rack belonging to Hirsch Brothers.* ______________________

____

3. *The bill for Slade* totaled twenty-one dollars and fifty cents. ______________________

____

4. Mr. Baumer saw Slade in front of *the door of the saloon.* ______________________

____

5. *The shifts of the two clerks* always increased before Christmas. ______________________

____

EXERCISE B **Revising Sentences with Contractions**

Rewrite the following sentences, replacing the italicized words with contractions.

EXAMPLE: *It is* important for Al to finish school. It's important for Al to finish school.

1. Mr. Baumer *does not* want to forget about Slade's bill. ______________________

____

2. If you let the freighters get away with stealing whiskey, *they will* do it every time. ______

____

3. *I am* able to work a few extra days if you need me to. ______________________

____

4. *I would* talk to the sheriff about Slade if I were you. ______________________

____

5. *There is* only one way to stop Slade. ______________________

____

Copyright © by Holt, Rinehart and Winston. All rights reserved.

NAME ______________________ CLASS ______________ DATE ____________

GRAMMAR LINK

Amigo Brothers

Piri Thomas

Pupil's Edition page 256

Punctuate Dialogue Correctly—And Punch Up Your Writing

VICTOR: Did you hear Joe say he was a boxer just like Felix and Antonio?

ANNA: Well, I heard him say, "I boxed in the school tournament."

Victor and Anna are saying similar things, but Victor is rewording Joe's statement while Anna is quoting Joe's exact words. Quotation marks are always used to enclose a direct quotation—a person's exact words. Do not use quotation marks to enclose an indirect quotation—a rewording of a direct quotation.

Keep the following rules in mind when you use quotation marks.

1. Begin a quoted remark with a capital letter.

"Don't you think Felix and Antonio have a great friendship?" he asked.

2. When a quoted sentence is interrupted, the second part of the sentence begins with a lowercase letter.

"Yes," I answered, **"**they are a real inspiration."

3. Use a comma, a question mark, or an exclamation point (never a period) to set off a quotation mark from the rest of the sentence.

INCORRECT: "I think so, too." he said.

CORRECT: "I think so, too**,"** he said.

4. Always put commas and periods inside the closing quotation marks.

"Starting tomorrow**,"** he said, "I'm going to be that open with my friends**."**

5. Question marks and exclamation points go inside the closing quotation marks if the quotation itself is a question or exclamation. Otherwise, they are placed outside.

"Don't you think that's a good idea**?"** he asked.

"It's a great idea**!"** I said, pretending to be excited.

I wonder why he said, "Starting tomorrow**"?**

Copyright © by Holt, Rinehart and Winston. All rights reserved.

EXERCISE A Identifying the Correct Punctuation for Dialogue

On the line before each item, write **C** if the punctuation and capitalization are correct. If the punctuation or capitalization is incorrect, write **I** and circle the error or errors. The sentences are based on events in "Amigo Brothers."

______ **1.** "You know, Felix," said Antonio, Maybe we're making too big a deal out of this."

______ **2.** "What do you mean"? he responded. "I never wanted to fight you"!

______ **3.** "I mean," said Antonio, "It would be a shame to force my best friend into a losing position."

NAME ______________________ CLASS ______________ DATE ____________

______ 4. Felix smiled. "Hey, man, what makes you so sure I'll lose?"

______ 5. "Self-confidence, I guess," answered Antonio. "My grandfather always used to say that if you don't have confidence in yourself, nobody else is going to have confidence in you!"

EXERCISE B Adding the Correct Punctuation for Dialogue

Correctly punctuate the following sentences by adding quotation marks, capital letters, and any necessary periods, commas, question marks, or exclamation points. The sentences are based on events in "Amigo Brothers."

EXAMPLE: "Did you hear about the big match?" asked Mr. Sayer.

1. Felix has got a dynamite punch, said Mr. Sayer. My money's on him
2. His friend thought about that for a moment. Yes, he said, but have you seen Tony move
3. These guys are amigo brothers, though, observed another man in the crowd. I heard one of them tell the other that he didn't really want to fight.
4. Mr. Sayer's face reddened. These boys are cheverote fighters. It will be a fair fight
5. The man certainly hadn't meant to imply a fixed fight when he said these guys are amigo brothers!

EXERCISE C Writing Dialogue

Rewrite the following sentences by changing them to direct quotations. The sentences are based on events in "Amigo Brothers."

EXAMPLE: Felix said they would get together after the fight.
Felix said, "We'll get together after the fight."

1. Felix told Antonio that he would be staying with his aunt Lucy. ______
2. Antonio wanted to know if Felix feels the same way he does about the fight. ______
3. Felix said he was really psyched up for the fight after seeing the movie. ______
4. Feeling lonely already, he shook Tony's hand and told him goodbye. ______
5. Antonio prayed for a quick knockout so that he would not hurt Felix too much. ______

Copyright © by Holt, Rinehart and Winston. All rights reserved.

NAME ______________________ CLASS ______________ DATE ____________

GRAMMAR LINK

Brian's Song

William Blinn

Pupil's Edition page 324

Transitions Make the Right Connection

> **PETRA (reading aloud her report):** As a result of rooming with Brian Piccolo, Gale Sayers loosened up. For example, Gale Sayers said that before he roomed with Brian he had never short-sheeted one of his other roommates' beds. Brian Piccolo wasn't all fun and games, however. He worked hard; consequently, he made Gale Sayers work hard.

How has Petra connected the ideas in her report so that it reads smoothly? She has used **transitional words and phrases** such as *as a result, for example, however,* and *consequently.* These words and phrases help link the ideas in her report.

Transitional words and phrases show how sentences in a paragraph relate to each other by showing contrast, cause and effect, and time order.

CONTRAST: Linda loved to watch Gale play football; **however,** she was always nervous that he might get hurt.

CAUSE AND EFFECT: Gale was tackled during the game. **As a result,** his knee was badly injured.

TIME ORDER: Brian made Gale lift weights; **finally,** he was able to run.

Make sure that the two sentences that are linked by a transition contain related ideas.

FAULTY TRANSITION: Brian played high school football. Furthermore, he had a bulldog named Fido.

EFFECTIVE TRANSITION: Brian played high school football. **Furthermore,** his bulldog Fido was the team's mascot.

With the exception of coordinating conjunctions like *and* and *but,* a transitional word or phrase that joins clauses is preceded by a semicolon and followed by a comma.

> Gale was fed up with Brian**; otherwise,** he wouldn't have put mashed potatoes and gravy on Brian's chair.

A transitional word or phrase that interrupts a clause is set off by two commas.

> Brian said**, finally,** that he would go to the hospital for tests.

Common Transitional Words and Phrases			
accordingly	finally	likewise	since
also	for example	meanwhile	then
although	furthermore	moreover	therefore
as a result	however	nevertheless	to begin with
because	in fact	on the other hand	thus
consequently	instead	otherwise	yet

Copyright © by Holt, Rinehart and Winston. All rights reserved.

NAME ______________________ CLASS ______________ DATE ____________

EXERCISE A Punctuating Transitional Phrases

Add the correct punctuation to each of the following sentences.

EXAMPLE: Brian tells Gale that Coach Halas is deaf in one ear; consequently, Gale tries to stay on the coach's good side.

1. Brian begins to lose weight and to cough as a result he goes into the hospital.
2. The fake draw, screen right for example is a football play that the Bears used.
3. Dick Butkus was a linebacker for Chicago furthermore he was a *big* linebacker!
4. Brian was caught talking consequently he had to sing a fight song in front of everyone.
5. Brian needed his rest therefore the nurse told Gale to leave.

EXERCISE B Using Transitional Words and Phrases to Link Ideas

Rewrite the sentences below so that the ideas are more closely connected. Use transitional words and phrases. You may create one or two sentences.

EXAMPLE: Players are fined for talking. They might keep talking and miss the important points the coaches are trying to make.

Players are fined for talking; otherwise, they might keep talking and miss the important points the coaches are trying to make.

1. Coach Halas noticed Brian's improvement. He made Brian the number one fullback.

____

____

2. Gale Sayers and Brian Piccolo roomed together. They didn't let the difference in the color of their skin bother them.

____

____

3. In one game, Brian carried the ball fourteen times for 105 yards. He was awarded the game ball.

____

____

4. Football can be a dangerous sport. A quarterback might injure his throwing arm.

____

____

5. Brian had one operation. He had to undergo another one.

____

____

Copyright © by Holt, Rinehart and Winston. All rights reserved.

NAME ______________________ CLASS ______________ DATE ____________

GRAMMAR LINK

User Friendly

T. Ernesto Bethancourt **Pupil's Edition page 366**

Pronouns Can Be Problems

RITA: Between you and I, I don't think Chuck likes Kevin.

LINDA: You mean, "Between you and me, Chuck doesn't like Kevin."

RITA: Yes, let's do keep it between us.

Why does Rita misunderstand what Linda is trying to tell her? Rita doesn't realize that the correct pronoun to use as the object of a preposition is *me,* not *I.* The following rules explain which pronouns to use as the subject of a sentence and which ones to use as the direct object, indirect object, or object of a preposition.

1. Use the pronouns *I, she, he, we,* or *they* when

(a) the pronoun is the subject of a verb in a sentence

EXAMPLES: **He** wanted a voice. [*He* is the subject of *wanted.*]
We both do like computers. [*We* is the subject of *do like.*]

(b) the pronoun follows a linking verb (such as *seem, feel, smell,* and all forms of the verb *be*) and refers to the subject

EXAMPLE: The object of Kevin's affection was **she.** [*She* follows the linking verb *was.*]

If sentences like the one above sound odd to you, turn them around in your mind.

EXAMPLE: **She** was the object of Kevin's affection.

2. When the pronoun is the direct object, the indirect object, or the object of a preposition in a sentence, use *me, her, him, us,* or *them.*

EXAMPLES: Louise loved **him.** [*Him* is the direct object of the verb *loved.*]
Kevin told the computer about **her.** [*Her* is the object of the preposition *about.*]

The pronoun rules listed above also apply when a pronoun is part of a compound subject or a compound object.

EXAMPLES: **He** and **I** built the computer.
Sports are important for **him** and **them.**

To help you choose the correct pronoun when using a compound subject or a compound object, try each form of the pronoun separately:

She and (*they, them*) attend Santa Rosario Junior High School.

Which is correct: *Them* attend Santa Rosario Junior High School, or *They* attend Santa Rosario Junior High School? When you try each pronoun separately, you can tell that *they* is the correct pronoun to use as the subject.

She and they attend Santa Rosario Junior High School.

Copyright © by Holt, Rinehart and Winston. All rights reserved.

NAME ______________________ CLASS ______________ DATE ____________

EXERCISE A Choosing Correct Pronoun Forms

Underline the personal pronoun in parentheses that correctly completes each of the following sentences.

EXAMPLES: I guess we know what she thinks of (*he*, *him*).
The only one at home was (*I*, *me*).

1. Wow! Louis's question certainly surprised (*I*, *me*).
2. Kevin hadn't ever spoken to (*she*, *her*).
3. Louis was concerned about (*he*, *him*) and his problems.
4. Louis would not give (*I*, *me*) a straight answer.
5. The Rangers' left tackle was (*he*, *him*).
6. Did (*she*, *her*) have any reason to suspect Kevin?
7. Louis was talking to other computers and learning from (*they*, *them*).
8. Then, (*they*, *them*) looked at the final printout.
9. The students who were most amazed by the ending were (*we*, *us*).
10. Could anything like that ever happen to (*we*, *us*)?

EXERCISE B Revising Sentences Using Correct Pronoun Forms

Each of the following sentences contains a personal pronoun in a compound subject or a compound object. If the personal pronoun is incorrect, rewrite the sentence correctly on the lines provided. If the personal pronoun is correct, write **C.**

EXAMPLE: On the bus, Kevin saw Ginny and they. On the bus, Kevin saw Ginny and them.

1. The students at the back of the bus are often Sherry and Linda or we. ______________
2. Will Ginny sit between Linda and I? ______________
3. Ginny's family and him had several upsetting surprises. ______________
4. Why did Louis wish to harm Chuck and she? ______________
5. Perhaps the engineers or them will find a bug in the program. ______________

Copyright © by Holt, Rinehart and Winston. All rights reserved.

NAME ______________________ CLASS ______________ DATE ____________

GRAMMAR LINK

Miss Awful

Arthur Cavanaugh **Pupil's Edition page 385**

Homonym Alert! Homonym Alert!

EVELYN: Why did Roger's mother want to talk to the *principal* about Miss Orville?

PACO: Because Miss Orville's methods offended Mrs. Clark's *principles*.

Why are the italicized words in the two sentences above spelled differently, even though they sound the same? These words are **homonyms,** which means that their pronunciations are the same but their meanings and spellings are different. The list below gives the spellings and meanings of some common homonyms. When you proofread, look for homonyms in your work; then check in a dictionary to see that you have used the correct spellings.

brake **break**	*n.,* a device to stop a machine *vt.,* to fracture; to shatter; to interrupt	I used the emergency *brake* to prevent the car from rolling downhill. Don't *break* that mirror.
waist **waste**	*n.,* the part of the body above the hips and below the ribs *vt.,* to spend or use carelessly	He pulled the belt tight around his *waist.* Classroom time is too valuable to *waste* daydreaming.
capital **capitol**	*n.,* a city that is the seat of government *n.,* statehouse building	What is the *capital* of this state? The *capitol* is on Congress Avenue.
coarse **course**	*adj.,* rough; crude; not fine *n.,* path of action; series of studies (also used in the expression *of course*)	The *coarse* sand acts as a filter. What is the best *course* for me to take? You may change your mind, of *course.*
council **counsel**	*n.,* a group of advisors or administrators *n.,* advice *vt.,* to advise	The mayor's *council* has seven members. He needs legal *counsel* on this matter. His attorney will *counsel* him before the hearing.
councilor **counselor**	*n.,* a member of a council *n.,* one who advises	The mayor appointed seven *councilors.* Mr. Jackson is the guidance *counselor* for the seventh grade.

Copyright © by Holt, Rinehart and Winston. All rights reserved.

NAME ______________________ CLASS ______________ DATE ____________

continued

principal	*n.*, the head of a school *adj.*, chief; main	The *principal* spoke of the *principal* duties of students.
principle	*n.*, rule of conduct; a fundamental truth	Action should be guided by *principle*.
stationary	*adj.*, in a fixed position	Is that chalkboard *stationary*?
stationery	*n.*, writing paper	Do you have any white *stationery*?

EXERCISE A Choosing Correct Homonyms

Each of the following sentences contains a pair of homonyms in parentheses. Underline the correct homonym for each sentence.

EXAMPLE: "We could hire legal (*council, counsel*) and sue her," said one student.

1. Some of Roger's classmates used (*course, coarse*) language to describe Miss Orville.
2. The eviction notice was written on official city (*stationary, stationery*).
3. Some of the parents wanted to complain to the (*principal, principle*).
4. Miss Orville asked a volunteer to name the (*capitol, capital*) city of the United States.
5. The school (*counselor, councilor*) and Miss Orville were talking in the hallway.
6. The city (*councilor, counselor*) was sympathetic but could not prevent the eviction.
7. Roger applied the (*break, brake*) and brought his bicycle to a halt.
8. Bending forward at the (*waist, waste*), the dance partners bowed to each other.
9. Form a (*stationery, stationary*) line, and do not move until I tell you.
10. The students destroyed the plant, but they did not (*break, brake*) the pot.

EXERCISE B Proofreading a Paragraph with Homonyms

The following paragraph is from an imaginary speech that Miss Orville might have given to the class. Proofread the paragraph and write the correct homonym above any word in the paragraph that is used incorrectly.

I have a fundamental principal that guides my teaching. Education is too valuable a treasure to waist. We should enjoy learning, of coarse. Write an educational goal on the official school stationary that I give you. If you need council, I will be happy to advise you. We will not take a brake until everyone has finished.

Copyright © by Holt, Rinehart and Winston. All rights reserved.

NAME ______________________ CLASS ______________ DATE ____________

GRAMMAR LINK

The Only Girl in the World for Me

Bill Cosby

Pupil's Edition page 392

Avoiding Unclear Pronoun References

CARLA: The girlfriend talked to the goddess when she got the note.

TED: When the girlfriend got the note, she talked to the goddess.

In the first sentence above, who got the note? We know from reading the story that the clause "when she got the note" refers to the girlfriend. However, Carla's sentence might confuse people who have not read the story. "Who got the note, the girlfriend or the goddess?" they might ask. In the second sentence, Ted makes it clear that *girlfriend* is the antecedent of the pronoun *she.*

Using a pronoun is such a way that it can refer to either of two antecedents produces an unclear reference. Below are some rules to keep in mind about exact pronoun references.

To avoid an unclear reference, make sure that a pronoun can refer to only one antecedent.

UNCLEAR: Though Bill must wait for Sidney, he is not discouraged. [Who is not discouraged, Bill or Sidney?]

CLEAR: Bill is not discouraged, though he must wait for Sidney.

UNCLEAR: Did the girlfriend tell the goddess each time she got a note? [Who got a note, the girlfriend or the goddess?]

CLEAR: Each time the girlfriend got a note, did she tell the goddess?

Using *it, they,* and *you* to refer to no particular person or thing produces an indefinite reference. Use *it, they,* and *you* only to refer to a particular person, place, idea, or thing.

INDEFINITE: In the selection it tells how the author met his first girlfriend. [The pronoun *it* does not refer to any particular thing.]

CLEAR: The selection tells how the author met his first girlfriend.

EXERCISE A Revising Unclear Pronoun References

Each of the following sentences contains an unclear pronoun reference. Revise each sentence to make the pronoun reference clear. Make sure that you include a specific antecedent for each pronoun you use.

EXAMPLE: Persistence can beat resistance if it is consistent.

If persistence is consistent, it can beat resistance.

1. Was Bill jealous of Sidney while he was going with the goddess? ______________

____

2. Bill thought of Romeo before he left his seat. ______________

____

Copyright © by Holt, Rinehart and Winston. All rights reserved.

3. People probably looked at Bill and the girl because they were curious. ____________

____

4. When Cupid's arrow struck Bill's heart, it was consumed with conquest. ____________

____

5. Cosby alludes to Mercury; he is the Roman god of messages. ____________

____

EXERCISE B Revising to Make Indefinite Pronoun References Clear

Each of the following sentences contains an indefinite pronoun reference. Revise each sentence to make the pronoun reference clear.

EXAMPLE: In the note, it described Bill as "cute."
The note described Bill as "cute."

1. In the first paragraph, it gives Cosby's age as twelve.

____

____

2. At Western Union, they send telegrams.

____

____

3. Apparently, in sixth grade you write notes, not make conversation.

____

____

4. At the beginning of *Love and Marriage,* it has a dedication to Camille.

____

____

5. *Romeo and Juliet* is appealing because they dramatize the fates of two young lovers.

____

____

Copyright © by Holt, Rinehart and Winston. All rights reserved.

NAME ______________________ CLASS ______________ DATE ___________

LANGUAGE LINK

Sky Woman

retold by Joseph Bruchac — **Pupil's Edition page 432**

Style: Avoiding Clichés

When Flint saw all the things that the Good Mind made, he was *green with envy.*

Did Flint actually turn green? Of course he didn't. Yet it wouldn't strike most readers that the comparison between Flint and the color green was in any way unusual. That's because the phrase *green with envy* is a **cliché**—an overworked expression that has lost its freshness and meaning. Clichés include expressions such as *busy as a bee, the crack of dawn, on top of the world,* and *eat like a horse*.

EXAMPLES: No matter how humid it is, Sky Woman always looks *fresh as a daisy.*
Leave no stone unturned as you try to do good things, not bad.

To find clichés in your own writing, look at your descriptions or comparisons and ask yourself if you've heard people make the same comparison many times before. If so, you're probably using a cliché. Avoid clichés by being direct or by thinking of a fresh, new comparison.

CLICHÉ: After their argument, Sky Woman and her daughter buried the hatchet.
DIRECT: After their argument, Sky Woman and her daughter **made up.**
NEW COMPARISON: After their argument, Sky Woman and her daughter **became like sisters once more.**

EXERCISE A Finding Clichés

Underline the cliché in each passage below.

1. "Accidents will happen—it wasn't my fault!" said Sky Woman's daughter.
2. "You'll live to regret this," said the chief as Sky Woman fell from Sky World.
3. Sky Woman's warnings to her daughter went in one ear and out the other.
4. "The nice things Flint does," said the Good Mind, "are few and far between. Getting him to say 'thank you' is harder than climbing Mount Everest in a single day."
5. Flint scowled. "Well, at least I do whatever I want to—not like the Good Mind, who's so good he bores me to tears."

EXERCISE B Revising Clichés

On the lines provided, rewrite each sentence, creating a new comparison or a more direct phrase to replace the cliché in italics. Do not change the basic meaning of each sentence.

EXAMPLE: I wouldn't trust Flint *further than I could throw him.*
I wouldn't trust Flint even if he had won the Nobel Peace Prize.

1. People in Sky World used to be *as happy as clams.* ______________________

____

Copyright © by Holt, Rinehart and Winston. All rights reserved.

NAME ______________________ CLASS ______________ DATE ____________

2. Things would have turned out much differently if the chief of Sky World had *had a change of heart.* ______________________________

____

3. Uprooting the Sky Tree made a hole *as big as a barn* in Sky Land. ______________________________

____

4. Sky Woman's daughter *grew like a weed.* ______________________________

____

5. Getting rid of Flint was *easier said than done.* ______________________________

____

EXERCISE C **Proofreading Paragraphs**

Underline five clichéd expressions in the paragraphs below, and rewrite each one in the space above it, using either a new comparison or a more direct phrase.

When Sky Woman fell through the hole in Sky Land, she didn't know which way to turn. Luckily, however, the animals decided to lend her a hand. They dredged up earth from the bottom of the sea, and Sky Woman used the land that grew out of it to plant seeds from the Sky Tree. Pretty soon, trees and plants were growing like crazy all over the new continent.

When she saw the way the animals had helped her, Sky Woman thought she might be able to be happy again. But with the birth of her grandsons, her troubles began afresh. One of her grandsons, the Good Mind, was as good as an angel, but Flint was always looking for trouble. He did everything he could to destroy all of the hard work that Sky Woman and the Good Mind had put into making their new home a pleasant place to live.

Copyright © by Holt, Rinehart and Winston. All rights reserved.

LANGUAGE LINK

When the Earth Shakes

Patricia Lauber **Pupil's Edition page 442**

Style: Formal and Informal English

MELISSA: Whoa, that quake was some kind of disaster!

LEIGH: Yes, it certainly was. I believe some scientists have determined that it registered 8.5 on the Richter scale.

If you read Melissa's and Leigh's statements aloud, you'll probably notice that they sound quite different. That's because Melissa is speaking *informal* English, whereas Leigh is speaking *formal* English. The language of formal English is thoughtful and precise. By contrast, the language of informal English is casual and conversational. It often includes **colloquialisms,** colorful everyday expressions, and slang. **Slang** consists of made-up words or old words used in new ways. Compare the formal and informal language in the chart below.

Informal	Formal
She doesn't have a clue.	She does not know.
You've got to be kidding me.	I do not believe you.
He took everything but the kitchen sink.	He took everything that could be taken.
They'll be there in a jiffy.	They will be there very soon.

Use formal English in reports, speeches, in your school writing assignments, and for other serious occasions. Most people use informal English in conversation, as when talking to their classmates, friends, and family members. You can also use informal English when writing to friends, or in your diary or journal. At times, it may be difficult to tell whether to use informal or formal English. In these cases, you will need to consider your audience and purpose before deciding how formal your own language should be.

EXERCISE A Choosing Words to Complete Sentences

For each of the following sentences, read the words in parentheses, and underline the formal English word or words to complete the sentence.

EXAMPLE: Seeing the destruction caused by the earthquake was (*a bummer, quite depressing*).

1. The (*young man, kid*) who worked in the flower shop felt lucky that he had left work early on the day of the earthquake.
2. However, he felt (*jerky, ashamed*) because of his behavior.
3. He was so (*terrified, freaked out*) that he could not return to town to help with cleanup efforts.
4. In fact, he felt (*positively, way*) ridiculous, because he had spent the night cowering in his cellar.
5. He hoped that no one would (*tease, dis*) him at work the next day.

Copyright © by Holt, Rinehart and Winston. All rights reserved.

NAME ______________________ CLASS ______________ DATE ______________

EXERCISE B Using Context to Determine Style

Rewrite each of the following sentences on the lines provided, using informal or formal English, according to what would be appropriate for the situation in parentheses.

EXAMPLE: We were relieved to discover that our car had not been damaged by the earthquake. *[Reword the sentence as a person might say it to a neighbor.]*

We were glad to find out that our car came out of the quake without a scratch.

1. You should check out the way that mountain split in half! *[Reword the sentence as a scientist might say it to a colleague.]* ______________________

2. Due to the layer of oil floating on the surface of the bay, flames from inland fires raced out into the sea. *[Reword the sentence as a high school student might explain it to a friend.]* ______________________

3. The enormous waves surged toward land, causing entire waterfronts to disappear in underwater landslides. *[Reword the sentence as an eyewitness might say it to an on-the-scene television reporter.]* ______________________

4. While the earthquake was going on, cars were bouncing on the streets like basketballs. *[Reword the sentence as an insurance agent might write it in a report to his company.]* ______________________

5. The tension in the earth released in earthquakes is sort of like when you yank on a bow and arrow and then let the string go. *[Reword the sentence as it might appear in a science textbook.]* ______________________

6. When the earthquake rolled through town, most folks in Turnagain were hanging out at home. *[Reword the sentence as it might appear in a newspaper article.]* ______________________

7. When the earthquake was over, most of the citizens of Turnagain discovered that their homes had been destroyed. *[Reword the sentence as a high school student might say it to a friend.]* ______________________

Copyright © by Holt, Rinehart and Winston. All rights reserved.

NAME ______________________ CLASS ______________ DATE ____________

LANGUAGE LINK

from Survive the Savage Sea

Dougal Robertson — **Pupil's Edition page 459**

Style: Active and Passive Voice

The Robertsons were saved by a Japanese fishing crew.

A Japanese fishing crew saved the Robertsons.

Both sentences describe the same event. However, the Robertsons are emphasized in the first sentence, whereas the Japanese fishing crew is emphasized in the second. The difference in stress comes from the fact that the verb in the first sentence is in the **passive voice,** while in the second the verb is written in the **active voice.** Verbs written in the active voice emphasize the *performer* of the action, while verbs written in the passive voice emphasize the *receiver* of the action.

A verb written in the passive voice is always a verb phrase that includes a form of the verb *be,* such as *is, are, was, were,* or *have been,* and the past participle of the main verb.

EXAMPLE: The Robertsons **were saved** by a Japanese fishing crew.

In this example, *were* is a form of the verb *be,* and *saved* is the past participle of the main verb.

Although writing in the passive voice is not grammatically incorrect, you should avoid overusing it. Verbs in the passive voice are weak because the performer of the action is revealed indirectly, if at all. Also, because it requires more words than the active voice to express a thought, the passive voice can be wordy and awkward.

AWKWARD PASSIVE: The sea turtle **was killed** by Dougal.
ACTIVE: Dougal **killed** the sea turtle.

The passive voice *can* be used in several cases:

- when you don't know who or what performed the action
  EXAMPLE: Somehow, a hole **was punched** in the raft.
- when you don't want to specify the performer of the action
  EXAMPLE: The food on the raft **was eaten** too quickly.
- when you want to emphasize the person or thing that received the action
  EXAMPLE: Dougal **was considered** a hero.

Generally, don't use the passive voice *unless* you have a good reason to use it.

EXERCISE A Identifying Active and Passive Voice

For each of the following sentences, decide whether the voice of the verb is active or passive. In the blank before the sentence, write **A** for active or **P** for passive.

EXAMPLE: ___P___ The journal was written on pieces of sail.

______ **1.** Water was rationed from the very beginning.

______ **2.** They used up their flares.

Copyright © by Holt, Rinehart and Winston. All rights reserved.

______ 3. Dougal, Lyn, and the children all took turns keeping watch.

______ 4. Flying fish were used to catch dorados.

______ 5. The dinghy and raft were tossed by churning waves in the storm.

EXERCISE B Changing Sentences from Passive to Active Voice

Each of the following sentences is in the passive voice. On the line below, rewrite the sentence to change the voice from passive to active. Do not change the basic meaning of the sentence.

EXAMPLE: The *Lucette* was destroyed by killer whales.

Killer whales destroyed the Lucette.

1. Sandy's spirits were lifted by Dougal's good humor.

____

2. Nothing was wasted by the Robertsons—not even turtle blood.

____

3. The situation was understood by the children to be very grave.

____

4. Their water supply was threatened by a lack of rain.

____

5. The hand-held flares were finally spotted by a Japanese fishing crew.

____

EXERCISE C Writing and Classifying Sentences

On the lines below, write five sentences about a shipwreck. Then, trade papers with a classmate. Circle the verbs in the active voice in your classmate's paragraph. Underline the verbs in the passive voice. There should be more verbs circled than underlined. If not, make suggestions for changing some of the passive verbs to active.

Copyright © by Holt, Rinehart and Winston. All rights reserved.

NAME ______________________ CLASS ______________ DATE ____________

LANGUAGE LINK

Antaeus

Borden Deal **Pupil's Edition page 481**

Style: Dialect—Voices of a Region or a Group

I ain't a-comin' with you nohow.

I'm not coming with you no matter what.

Which of the sentences above would you expect T. J. to say? Which would you expect the narrator of "Antaeus" to say? Although both of these sentences are informal in tone and style, they are distinguishable. The first uses words, expressions, and syntax that mark it as coming from a particular region—the Southern United States. The second sentence uses words and syntax familiar to everyone who speaks English. A form of a language used by a particular group of people is called a **dialect.**

A dialect shared by people from the same area of a country is called a **regional dialect.** T. J., for example, speaks in Southern dialect. People from other areas of the country also have specialized dialects. For instance, people born and raised in New England tend to speak differently than native Californians.

The variety of English most people use at school and work is **standard American English.** It is the form of English most often used in books and magazines and on radio and television. Language that doesn't follow the rules and guidelines of standard English is called **nonstandard English.**

NONSTANDARD ENGLISH: I ain't never been horseback ridin' afore.

STANDARD ENGLISH: I haven't ever been horseback riding before.

EXERCISE A Identifying Dialect

The following phrases have been taken from "Antaeus." Decide whether each is in a dialect or is in standard American English. In the blank before the sentence, write **D** for dialect or **S** for standard American English.

______ **1.** "That's all the name I got."

______ **2.** "He just moved into the building yesterday."

______ **3.** ". . . you get part of the bale offen your acre."

______ **4.** "We didn't really know what he was talking about . . ."

______ **5.** "It was mine to plant and make ever' year."

______ **6.** "You'd have to be a good farmer to make these tar roofs grow any watermelons."

______ **7.** ". . . he reckoned a few more weeks ought to see the job through."

______ **8.** "I ain't never put no effort into that."

______ **9.** "I spent all my life trying not to raise grass."

______ **10.** "He knew where to give in."

From "Antaeus" by Borden Deal. Copyright © 1961 by Southern Methodist University Press. Reprinted by permission of ***Ashley Deal Matin.***

Copyright © by Holt, Rinehart and Winston. All rights reserved.

NAME ______________________ CLASS ______________ DATE ____________

EXERCISE B Rewriting Dialect as Standard American English

On the lines provided, rewrite the following dialect sentences from "Antaeus" in standard American English.

1. "Don't you-all have no woods around here?"

2. "You mean you ain't got no fields to raise nothing in?"

3. "Come spring we could raise us what we want to—watermelons and garden truck and no telling what all."

4. "Then you lay it by . . . and then you got you a crop."

5. "You-all seem mighty set on raising some grass."

6. "I got a quarter. How much you-all got?"

7. ". . . we're just fixing to plant us some watermelon."

8. "They'd be mighty nice to eat while we was a-laying on that grass."

9. "You ain't got no right."

10. "Can't nobody touch a man's own land."

Copyright © by Holt, Rinehart and Winston. All rights reserved.

LANGUAGE LINK

The Origin of the Seasons

retold by Olivia Coolidge **Pupil's Edition page 511**

Style: Descriptive Language

Vivid verbs, nouns, and adjectives are ingredients of good descriptive writing. You can add to your bank of descriptive words by taking verbs you already know and turning them into verb forms that can act as adjectives and nouns, as in the following examples.

> Hades struggled with the **terrified** girl.
>
> **Weeping** made her eyes red.

In the first sentence above, *terrified,* a form of the verb *terrify,* is acting as an adjective. In the second, *weeping,* a form of the verb *weep,* is acting as a noun.

When a verb becomes an adjective, like *terrified,* it is called a **participle.** There are two kinds of participles: present participles and past participles.

Present participles are verb forms ending in *-ing* that can be used as adjectives.

> Hades watched the *laughing* girl. [*Laughing,* a form of the verb *laugh,* acts as an adjective modifying the noun *girl.*]

Past participles are verb forms, generally ending in *-ed* or *-d,* that can be used as adjectives.

> The *kidnapped* girl cried for her mother. [*Kidnapped,* a form of the verb *kidnap,* acts as an adjective modifying the noun *girl.*]

When a verb is used as a noun, it is called a **gerund.** A gerund is formed by adding *-ing* to a verb. A gerund can take any position in a sentence that a noun can. Gerunds are often used as subjects, as objects of prepositions, or as direct objects.

SUBJECT:	*Searching* made Demeter exhausted.
OBJECT OF PREPOSITION:	Persephone was exhausted from *struggling.*
OBJECT OF VERB:	Demeter enjoyed *baby-sitting.*

EXERCISE A Identifying Participles and Gerunds

If the italicized word in the sentence is a gerund, write **G** in the space provided. If the italicized word is a participle, write **P** in the space and draw an arrow to the word the participle modifies.

EXAMPLE: __P__ The *horrified* mother grabbed her child.

______ **1.** Hades, *pleading,* asked Zeus for a wife.

______ **2.** *Disappointed* farmers stared at their dry fields.

______ **3.** *Worrying* made her old and gray.

______ **4.** Demeter has a sweet, *caring* nature.

______ **5.** Each year, Demeter's *mourning* results in winter weather.

Copyright © by Holt, Rinehart and Winston. All rights reserved.

NAME ______________________ CLASS ______________ DATE __________

EXERCISE B Writing Sentences with Participles and Gerunds

On the lines provided, write a sentence correctly using the form indicated in parentheses.

EXAMPLE: wilt (as a participle) The wilted flowers fell from her hand.

1. parch (as a participle)
2. eat (as a gerund)
3. scream (as a participle)
4. complain (as a gerund)
5. trap (as a participle)
6. sing (as a gerund)
7. encourage (as a participle)
8. run (as a participle)
9. wander (as a gerund)
10. ruin (as a participle)

Copyright © by Holt, Rinehart and Winston. All rights reserved.

NAME ______________________________ CLASS ________________ DATE ____________

LANGUAGE LINK

Orpheus, the Great Musician

retold by Olivia Coolidge **Pupil's Edition page 520**

Style: Figurative Language

The seasons *are like a wheel.*

Eurydice *is youth and hope.*

The earth *wept* for Orpheus.

What do the italicized words and phrases in the sentences above have in common? They are all forms of figurative language. Figurative language describes one thing in terms of another and is not literally true. Writers and speakers often use figurative language to create vivid word pictures. Figurative language can also help to make difficult ideas and concepts clearer. The following chart shows three major kinds of figurative language.

Figurative Language	Examples
Similes use the words *like, as,* or *than* to make a comparison.	• Without Eurydice, Orpheus is *like a lost lamb.* • Charon is *as gray as a ghost.* • Orpheus's grief is *deeper than the ocean.*
Metaphors make a comparison without using *like, as,* or *than.*	• Orpheus *is a lost lamb.* • Grief *is a deep ocean.*
Personification gives human qualities to nonhuman things.	• The river *growled angrily.* • The daffodils *bowed their heads in sorrow.*

EXERCISE A Identifying Figurative Language

On the line provided, write *simile, metaphor,* or *personification* to identify the type of figurative language in each sentence.

EXAMPLE: personification The myth *dared me to learn its meaning.*

_______________ 1. Myths are like doors to the past.

_______________ 2. The flames were hissing serpents.

_______________ 3. Sunlight smiled on the lovers.

_______________ 4. Eurydice is all of our lost loves.

_______________ 5. His doubt was a powerful magnet pulling him back.

_______________ 6. The trees sang as the cool breeze blew through their branches.

_______________ 7. Eurydice's eyes were bluer than pools of water.

_______________ 8. The underworld was as calm as the sea.

Copyright © by Holt, Rinehart and Winston. All rights reserved.

________________ **9.** The clouds threatened angrily as Orpheus descended into the world.

________________ **10.** The cave leading to the underworld was like the mouth of a giant beast.

EXERCISE B Using Figurative Language

Describe music and the underworld in several ways by completing the following word webs. In each circle, write a comparison using an example of the figurative language named in the circle. Examples are given to get you started.

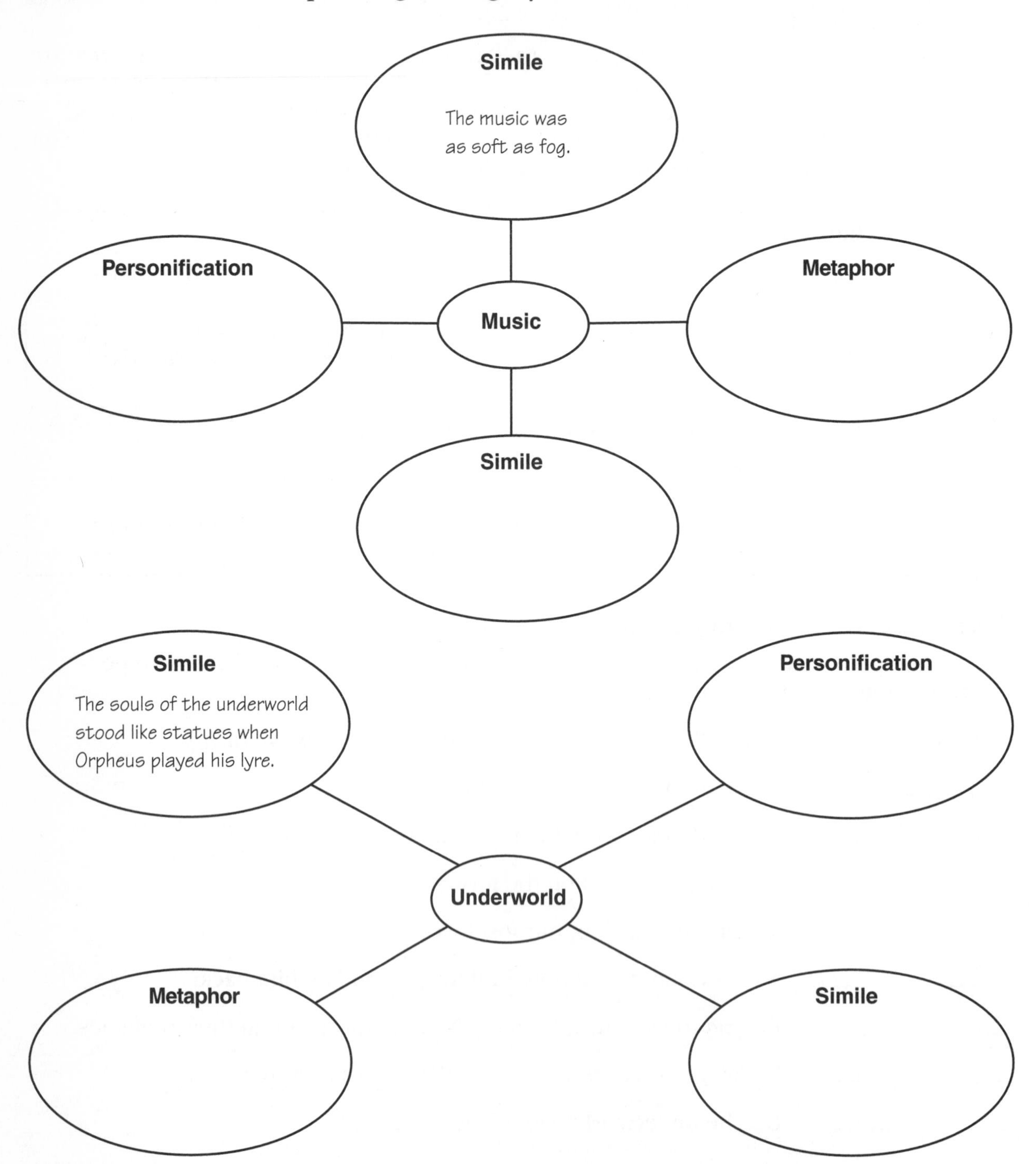

Copyright © by Holt, Rinehart and Winston. All rights reserved.

NAME ______________________ CLASS ______________ DATE ______________

GRAMMAR LINK

Echo and Narcissus

retold by Roger Lancelyn Green **Pupil's Edition page 529**

Words That Are Often Confused

"**Who's** there?" asked the traveler.

". . . there," came the answer.

"**Whose** voice is that?" the traveler wondered.

Notice that the boldface words above sound just alike when you say them aloud. However, they are spelled differently, and they serve different purposes.

Who's is a *contraction,* a shortened form of a pronoun and the verb *is, has,* or *are.* [*Who is* there?] A contraction *always* has an apostrophe.

Whose is a *possessive relative pronoun.* [To whom does that voice belong?] The following chart shows two other like-sounding pairs of contractions and possessive pronoun forms.

Possessive Pronoun Forms	Contractions
Its The tree sheds *its* leaves. [The leaves belong to the tree.]	**It's** *It's* autumn. [*It is* autumn.]
Your Can you see *your* reflection? [The reflection belongs to you.]	**You're** *You're* quite conceited! [*You are* quite conceited!]

If you are unsure which word is correct, try substituting the two words that make up the contraction in the sentence, such as *it is, who is,* or *you are,* and decide whether the sentence still makes sense.

EXAMPLE: Do you see *whose/who's* there?
Do you see *who is* there?

After substituting the two words that make up the contraction, it is easier to see in the example above that *who's* is the proper choice.

EXERCISE A Choosing Correct Words

Circle the word in parentheses that correctly completes each sentence.

EXAMPLE: Echo, (*you're,* *your*) love for Narcissus is doomed.

1. Narcissus, (*you're, your*) certainly in love with yourself!

2. (*It's, Its*) a fine day in the mountains.

3. A cloud casts (*it's, its*) shadow over the pool.

4. Echo knows (*who's, whose*) lost in the woods.

Copyright © by Holt, Rinehart and Winston. All rights reserved.

5. She is a nymph (*who's, whose*) love knows no bounds.

6. Narcissus, did you ever find (*you're, your*) true love?

7. (*It's, Its*) such a pretty flower.

8. (*Who's, Whose*) repeating everything I say?

9. (*You're, Your*) going to have to accept your fate, Echo.

10. The flower tips (*it's, its*) head toward the pool of water.

EXERCISE B **Proofreading a Paragraph**

In the paragraph below, there are errors in the use of pronouns and contractions. Circle each error, and write the correct form above it. The first error is identified and corrected as an example. You should find ten more.

it's

I think (its) fun to hear voices echo. You shout your message across a ravine, and your sure to hear part of it return. You hear the sound the first time when the sound waves reach you're ears by the most direct route. Then, if the sound also hits a large object like a building, it's waves bounce back, and you hear them a second time. When you hear the sound a second time, its an echo. Even though you know its just sound waves bouncing back, whose sure? At night when you're imagination runs wild and the moon hides it's face, you might wonder if it's Echo herself who's voice calls out, "Whose that?"

Copyright © by Holt, Rinehart and Winston. All rights reserved.

NAME ______________________ CLASS ______________ DATE ____________

GRAMMAR LINK

The Flight of Icarus

retold by Sally Benson **Pupil's Edition page 539**

Adjective vs. Adverb

He headed toward the sun.

He headed **swiftly** toward the **brilliant** sun.

What is it about the second sentence above that makes it more descriptive than the first? The addition of the adverb *swiftly* and the adjective *brilliant* modifies the sentence.

Adverbs are used to modify verbs, adjectives, or other adverbs. Adverbs tell *where, when, how,* or *to what extent.* In the sentence above, the adverb *swiftly* modifies the verb *headed.*

Where?	Fly *up* to the clouds. Put it *here.*
When?	It happened *yesterday.* He arrived *later.*
How?	They worked *quickly.* He soared *easily.*
To what extent? **(how often)** **(how long)**	Daedalus *always* remembered his son. *Briefly,* he felt the sun.

Adjectives are used to modify nouns or pronouns. An adjective modifies a word by telling *what kind, which one, how much,* or *how many.*

What kind?	He flew on *bright* wings.
Which one(s)	*Those* feathers came off.
How many?	There were *two* wings.
How much?	There was *little* time.

Adverbs are often formed by adding *-ly* to adjectives. In order to tell whether you need to add an *-ly* to a modifier to turn it into an adverb, ask yourself which word is modified. If the word modified is a verb, an adjective, or another adverb, then add *-ly.*

ADVERB: They stopped *quickly.* [The adverb *quickly* modifies the verb *stopped.*]

ADJECTIVE: They had a *quick* visit. [The adjective *quick* modifies the noun *visit.*]

EXERCISE A Identifying Adjectives and Adverbs

On the line provided, write **adjective** if the italicized word is an adjective, or **adverb** if it is an adverb. Then, draw an arrow to the word that the italicized word modifies.

EXAMPLE: ___adverb___ He flew *too* close to the sun.

______________ **1.** Icarus listened *carefully* to his father.

Copyright © by Holt, Rinehart and Winston. All rights reserved.

______________ **2.** His father was *cautious.*

______________ **3.** He attached *several* feathers to the frame.

______________ **4.** The boy was *almost* there.

______________ **5.** *Worrying,* he called his son back.

EXERCISE B Choosing Adjectives or Adverbs

Circle the word in parentheses that correctly completes each sentence.

EXAMPLE: Icarus soared (*easy,* *easily*) above the island.

1. Daedalus explained the route (*calm, calmly*).

2. The feathers fit (*perfect, perfectly*) on the frame.

3. The wax melted (*quick, quickly*) in the sun.

4. Daedalus's gaze was (*mournful, mournfully*) as he looked at the boy.

5. The end was sudden and (*swift, swiftly*).

EXERCISE C Writing Sentences Using Adverbs and Adjectives

On the line next to each word below, identify the word as either an adjective or an adverb. Then, write a sentence using the word correctly.

1. heavy ______________

____

____

2. slowly ______________

____

____

3. often ______________

____

____

4. quietly ______________

____

____

5. happy ______________

____

____

Copyright © by Holt, Rinehart and Winston. All rights reserved.

NAME ______________________ CLASS ______________ DATE ____________

GRAMMAR LINK

The Labors of Hercules

retold by Rex Warner

Pupil's Edition page 553

Do a *Good* Job with *Good* and *Well*

SUSANNA: "The Labors of Hercules" is a **good** story.

SYLVIA: Yes, Hercules performs his tasks **well.**

Good and *well* are both used correctly in the sentences above, but what is the difference between the two? Perhaps we should add a thirteenth labor to the twelve labors of Hercules: mastering the use of *good* and *well.*

Good is always an adjective. Use it to modify a noun or pronoun. Susanna correctly uses *good* to modify the noun *story.*

Well is usually an adverb. Use it to modify a verb, an adjective, or another adverb. Sylvia correctly uses *well* to modify the verb *performed.*

Before deciding whether to use *good* or *well,* figure out whether the word that you want to modify is a noun, a pronoun, a verb, an adjective, or an adverb. If the modified word is a noun or a pronoun, use *good.* If it is a verb, an adjective, or an adverb, use *well.*

NOUN: Hercules had **good** ideas.

VERB: Hercules did **well** with his assignments.

ADJECTIVE: The monster was **well** hidden in the woods.

Although *well* is usually an adverb, it can be used as an adjective to mean *healthy.*

EXAMPLE: After recovering from his wounds, Hercules felt **well** again.

You can use the expression *feel good* when you mean *feel happy or pleased.*

EXAMPLE: Did Hercules **feel good** about conquering monsters?

EXERCISE A Choosing *Good* or *Well*

For each sentence, write the correct word—*good* or *well*—on the line provided.

EXAMPLE: Eurystheus did not rule his kingdom ____well____.

1. Hercules is a ______________ example of a superhero.
2. He performed his amazing tasks ______________.
3. I feel sick, not ______________, looking at the gory remains of monsters.
4. Poor Hercules didn't feel ______________ about killing Chiron.
5. Hercules was ______________ armed with a giant club.

Copyright © by Holt, Rinehart and Winston. All rights reserved.

NAME ______________________ CLASS ______________ DATE ____________

EXERCISE B Proofreading Sentences

Read each sentence below. If *good* or *well* is used correctly, write **C** in the space provided. If *good* or *well* is used incorrectly, rewrite the sentence to make it correct.

EXAMPLE: I hope I do good on the test.

I hope I do well on the test.

1. Diana cared good for her sacred stag. ______________________

2. How good have you read this story? ______________________

3. Though the Hydra was well protected, Hercules conquered it. ______________________

4. Theseus didn't feel good about being in the underworld. ______________________

5. After a long rest, he felt good again. ______________________

6. Eurystheus thought Hercules performed each task a little too good. ______________________

7. Hercules was well taught by Chiron. ______________________

8. Eurystheus wasn't sure if bringing the savage mares to his palace was a well idea. ______________________

9. Hippolyte fought good, but she was no match for Hercules. ______________________

10. The nymphs of the river Po gave Hercules good advice. ______________________

Copyright © by Holt, Rinehart and Winston. All rights reserved.

NAME ______________________ CLASS ______________ DATE ______________

LANGUAGE LINK

King Midas and the Golden Touch

retold by Pamela Oldfield **Pupil's Edition page 564**

Style: Allusions

After reading the stories in Collection Seven, you can probably define the boldface words in the following sentences.

ALLUSION: The bodybuilder is aiming for a **Herculean** physique.
TRANSLATION: He wants to be as muscular as Hercules.

ALLUSION: She plays the guitar as if she were **Orpheus.**
TRANSLATION: She plays the guitar really well!

The boldface words above are **allusions.** An allusion is a word or phrase that refers to something or someone from literature, history, art, or some other branch of culture. For example, in the following sentence, an allusion is made to someone in mythology.

What a **narcissistic** person he is!

Since you have read the story of Narcissus, the allusion is clear to you and you can catch the meaning of the sentence.

EXERCISE A Completing Allusions

Complete each of the following sentences by writing the most appropriate name in the space provided.

Cerberus **Echo** **Midas** **Persephone** **Icarus** **Hercules**

EXAMPLE: He's foolhardy, and like Icarus he's going to take a fall.

1. She's a lovesick ______________, following that guy around all the time.
2. I don't want to be like ______________ and lose my family for years!
3. He's got a watchdog as protective as ______________.
4. If you can lift that piano, you're ______________!
5. Don't get greedy, or you may end up like ______________.

EXERCISE B Translating Allusions

On the lines provided, rewrite each sentence to show what the italicized allusion means.

EXAMPLE: That job is like *cleaning the Augean stables.*
That's an almost impossible job.

1. She's lucky with money, as if she *had the golden touch.* ______________________________

____

Copyright © by Holt, Rinehart and Winston. All rights reserved.

2. Don't go there, because it's *the underworld!* ______________

3. You'd have to be a *Hydra* to figure out all these answers at once. ______________

4. He's got a *Zeus-like attitude* that turns people off. ______________

5. From the expression on her face, you'd think she'd just seen *Eurydice.* ______________

EXERCISE C Creating Allusions

Now that you have become familiar with mythological allusions, create some allusions of your own. For each of the qualities listed below, write a sentence making an allusion to a familiar person, place, or thing.

EXAMPLE: smart He was a regular Albert Einstein.

1. tall ______________

2. small ______________

3. rich ______________

4. big ______________

5. musically talented ______________

6. fast ______________

7. dedicated ______________

8. funny ______________

Copyright © by Holt, Rinehart and Winston. All rights reserved.

NAME ______________________ CLASS ______________ DATE ____________

GRAMMAR LINK

Aesop's Fables

Pupil's Edition page 577

Bad or *Badly*?

Frog #1: This is a **bad** situation!
Frog #2: I was hoping that cranes thought frogs tasted **bad.**
Frog #3: Well, the log acted **badly** as a king, too.

In the sentences above, all the boldface words are used correctly. The following rules explain why.

Bad is an adjective and is used to describe a noun.

EXAMPLE: Asking for a new king was a **bad** idea.

Bad can also be used after verbs that name the senses, such as *feel, smell, taste, look,* and *sound.*

EXAMPLE: Your engine sounds **bad.**

Badly is an adverb. Use it to modify verbs, adjectives, or other adverbs.

MODIFYING A VERB: The crane acted **badly.**

MODIFYING AN ADJECTIVE: We don't need **badly** behaved kings! In this sentence, *behaved* is a participle, a verb form used as an adjective. *Badly behaved* describes the kings.

MODIFYING AN ADVERB: We've fallen **badly** behind the others in the race!

EXERCISE A Choosing *Bad* or *Badly*

In each sentence, write the correct word—*bad* or *badly*—in the space provided.

EXAMPLE: The Fox decided that the grapes tasted ____bad____.

1. The wolf wanted ______________ to catch a sheep.
2. City food smelled ______________ to the Country Mouse.
3. The Fox dealt with his disappointment ______________.
4. The boy didn't get any ______________ needed help.
5. The young Mouse felt ______________ about his silly idea.
6. The Country Mouse had a ______________ time in the city.
7. The Fox had a ______________ attitude.
8. The Mice ______________ needed a better solution to their problem.
9. The Fox decided that the grapes probably tasted ______________.
10. The Frog's decision was ______________ thought out.

Copyright © by Holt, Rinehart and Winston. All rights reserved.

NAME ______________________ CLASS ______________ DATE ____________

EXERCISE B **Proofreading a Story**

The story below contains errors in the use of *bad* and *badly.* Circle each error; then, write the correct word above the error. The first error is identified and corrected as an example. You should find five more errors.

badly

In the fable "The Dog and the Bone," a hungry dog needs a meal very bad. He finally finds an old bone, and though it smells badly, he quickly grabs it. He feels badly that he can't eat it right away, but another badly starved dog might see him.

Homeward the dog trots until he comes to a bad swollen stream. The dog looks into the water and sees his reflection. But with his bad eyesight, he thinks he is seeing another dog.

"That dog has a bone that's better than mine, and I want it bad!" thinks our hero. "I'll bark at him and scare him so bad that he'll drop the bone and leave it to me."

Of course, when the dog opens his mouth to bark, he loses the bone he already has. "Bad bone day," he mumbles, as he heads home.

Copyright © by Holt, Rinehart and Winston. All rights reserved.

NAME ______________________ CLASS ________________ DATE ____________

GRAMMAR LINK

Aschenputtel, retold by Jakob and Wilhelm Grimm

translated by Lucy Crane **Pupil's Edition page 606**

All Right, A Lot, Should Have, and *Would Have*

Dear Fairy Godmother,

Thanks for introducing me to Aschenputtel. I think that she and I are **alot** alike. You **should of** introduced me to her in time for the anniversary party for Prince Charming and me. I **would of** invited her and her prince. I guess it will be **alright** to invite her next year instead. Thanks again for making me who I am today.

Love, Cinderella

Can you see that Cinderella's letter has some spelling and grammatical problems? She seems to have forgotten the following writing rules.

- *A lot* and *all right* are always written as two words.
- *Should* and *would* are helping verbs that may be followed by the word *have*, but should never be followed by *of*.

The following chart shows other common spelling and usage errors and the corresponding correct spelling or usage.

Nonstandard	Standard	Example
could of	could have	Only birds **could have** picked up those lentils so quickly.
ought to of	ought to have	Her father **ought to have** been aware of her stepmother's cruelty.
might of	might have	The prince **might have** danced with someone else if Aschenputtel had not gone to the ball.
must of	must have	That girl **must have** lost her slipper.
anywheres everywheres nowheres somewheres	anywhere everywhere nowhere somewhere	The prince could not find Aschenputtel **anywhere.** He looked **everywhere.** She was **nowhere** to be found. Aschenputtel went **somewhere** where no one could find her.
hisself	himself	The prince took it upon **himself** to find Aschenputtel.
how come	why	Aschenputtel wished she understood **why** her stepmother was so cruel.
kind of sort of	somewhat rather	The stepsisters were **rather** jealous of Aschenputtel's marriage.
reason . . . because	reason . . . that	The **reason** Aschenputtel is rewarded is **that** she is a good person.
use to	used to	Aschenputtel **used to** have to clean out the fireplace.

Copyright © by Holt, Rinehart and Winston. All rights reserved.

NAME ________________ CLASS ________________ DATE ________________

EXERCISE A Rewriting Sentences

Each of the following sentences contains an error in usage. Circle each error, and rewrite the sentence correctly on the line provided.

EXAMPLE: The reason I like this story is (because) it has a happy ending.
The reason I like this story is that it has a happy ending.

1. Aschenputtel's stepsisters ought to of been nicer to her. ________________

2. Her stepmother wouldn't let her go anywheres, not even to the festival. ________________

3. The prince sat by hisself until the beautiful girl entered the festival. ________________

4. In her golden gown Aschenputtel looked sort of like a foreign princess. ________________

5. The prince didn't understand how come Aschenputtel was running away. ________________

EXERCISE B Proofreading Paragraphs

The following paragraphs contain errors in spelling or usage. Circle each error, and write your correction in the space above the line. The first error has been corrected for you as an example. You should find eight more errors.

used to
I (use to) think that "Cinderella" was just a movie. Now I know that it is a fairy tale known nearly everywheres in the world. By reading "Aschenputtel," I learned that fairy tales come in alot of different versions. This version of "Cinderella" might of been lost if the Brothers Grimm hadn't written it down.

My favorite part of "Aschenputtel" is the ending. The reason I like the end is because it shows why it's important to be a good person. The story is pretty violent, but in a fairy tale, that's alright. If it were a true story, it could of been pretty scary. I guess that's how come people like fairy tales so much. People sort of like to hear stories about good and evil, especially when there are happy endings.

Copyright © by Holt, Rinehart and Winston. All rights reserved.

NAME ________________ CLASS ________________ DATE ________________

GRAMMAR LINK

The Algonquin Cinderella, retold by M. R. Cox
Yeh-Shen, retold by Ai-Ling Louie

Pupil's Edition page 624

Two, To, and *Too*

Cassandra's Reading Log

Today I read two Cinderella stories. Tomorrow I am going to read one more. I wonder if I could be a Cinderella character, too. The next time that I go to a ball, I'll have to look out for my Prince Charming.

Why are words that sound the same spelled three different ways in the paragraph above? *Two* refers to a number. *To* is used as part of the infinitives "to read" and "to look" and as a preposition. *Too* means "also." The following chart shows the different spellings and uses of words that are often confused, like *two, to,* and *too.*

two	adjective	a number; one plus one Oochigeaskw had **two** sisters.
to	part of an infinitive; preposition	Yeh-Shen had **to** find her missing shoe. Her stepmother wouldn't let her go **to** the festival.
too	adverb	also; more than enough The Algonquins had a Cinderella story **too.** Her stepsister's foot was **too** big to fit the sandal.
accept	verb	to receive; to agree to She tried to **accept** her work without complaining.
except	preposition	with the exclusion of; but No one could see the Invisible One **except** his sister.
affect	verb	to act upon; to change How did her mother's death **affect** Yeh-Shen?
effect	noun	result; consequence Yeh-Shen's beauty had a dazzling **effect.**
already	adverb	previously Many women had **already** tried to see him.
all ready		all prepared They were **all ready** for the festival.
altogether	adverb	entirely The stepmother was **altogether** opposed to Yeh-Shen's attendance at the ball.
all together		everyone or everything in the same place The king and his men were **all together** as they searched for the slipper's owner.
than	conjunction	used in comparisons One sister was meaner **than** the other.
then	adverb	at that time He walked into the wigwam, **then** Oochigeaskw saw him.

Copyright © by Holt, Rinehart and Winston. All rights reserved.

NAME ______________________ CLASS ______________ DATE ____________

continued

weather	noun	the condition of the atmosphere The **weather** was beautiful for the festival.
whether	conjunction	if Yeh-Shen didn't know **whether** or not she could reveal her identity.

EXERCISE A Identifying Correct Usage

For each of the following sentences, read the words in parentheses and circle the word that correctly completes the sentence.

EXAMPLE: She went (*two,* (*to*), *too*) the festival against her stepmother's wishes.

1. Yeh-Shen had (*already, all ready*) put on the magic slipper.
2. No one recognized her (*accept, except*) her stepsister.
3. The stepmother thought she was (*altogether, all together*) too beautiful to be Yeh-Shen.
4. Yeh-Shen was wearing (*two, to, too*) beautiful golden slippers.
5. When she lost her shoe, she lost the magical (*affect, effect*) that it had produced.

EXERCISE B Proofreading a Paragraph

The following paragraph contains errors in spelling and/or phrasing. Circle the errors, and write corrections in the space above the line. The first error has been corrected for you as an example. You should find ten more errors.

weather

Oochigeaskw and the Invisible One were married in the fall, before the cold (whether) began. The people of the village were altogether before the lake, accept for Oochigeaskw's sisters, who were two ashamed to come to the wedding. They had been quite strongly effected by the news of their sister's good fortune. At first they were jealous, but than they began to see the error of their ways. The mean older sister was not all together mean, after all. She wished that she had acted differently and wondered weather she ought to apologize. But she thought she had been to mean to ever be forgiven. Oochigeaskw, however, wished for her sisters too attend her wedding. She went to find her sisters, and they were happy to except her kind invitation.

Copyright © by Holt, Rinehart and Winston. All rights reserved.

NAME ______________________ CLASS ______________ DATE ____________

GRAMMAR LINK

Oni and the Great Bird

retold by Abayomi Fuja **Pupil's Edition page 637**

They're, Their, There

Reading Quiz in Mr. Mendoza's Class:

MR. MENDOZA: How do Oni's friends react when they see his powers?

AMANDA: **They're** afraid of him.

MR. MENDOZA: Because the villagers are afraid of him, what do they do?

AMANDA: The villagers banish him from **their** village.

MR. MENDOZA: What does it mean to be banished?

AMANDA: It means Oni can never go back **there.**

What is special about the three words in boldface above? They are **homonyms,** which means they all sound the same, but they are used and spelled differently. The chart below gives the spelling and meaning of some common homonyms. How these words are spelled depends on how they are being used.

they're **their** **there**	[contraction of *they are*] [possessive form of *they*] [adverb] at that place [used to begin a sentence]	The people don't like Oni because **they're** afraid. Why did the eagle attack **their** town? Why do the people of Ajo keep living **there**? **There** was an abandoned canoe by a great river.
hear **here**	[verb] to receive sounds through the ears [adverb] in this place	They **hear** the giant eagle that terrorizes the town. **Here** Oni meets the king of Ajo.
peace **piece**	[noun] quiet order and security [noun] a part of something	Once again, **peace** reigned in the village of Ajo. Which **piece** of Oni's clothing was gone?
plain **plane**	[noun] a flat area of land [adjective] unadorned, simple [noun] a flat surface; a tool; an airplane	Oni travels over many a valley and **plain.** Did Oni use **plain,** ordinary arrows? How are a bird's wing and a **plane**'s wing shaped alike?
shone **shown**	[verb past tense of *shine*] [verb, past participle of *show*]	Anodo the eagle did not come out when the sun **shone.** The king was **shown** the magic boot.
threw **through**	[verb, past tense of *throw*] [preposition]	His neighbors **threw** him out of town. The eagle soared **through** the sky.
weak **week**	[adjective] feeble, not strong [noun] seven days	Others had been too **weak** to defeat the eagle. What a **week** Oni had!

Copyright © by Holt, Rinehart and Winston. All rights reserved.

NAME ______________________ CLASS ______________ DATE ____________

EXERCISE A Choosing Words to Complete Sentences

For each of the following sentences, read the words in parentheses and circle the word that correctly completes the sentences.

EXAMPLE: What did Oni find (*they're, their, there*) in the town of Ajo?

1. You might think that having magic boots would be a (*peace, piece*) of luck.
2. Did the canoe maker use a (*plain, plane*) to fashion the boat?
3. The people of Ajo feared (*they're, their, there*) common enemy, Anodo.
4. The Cinderella tale has been (*shone, shown*) to exist all over the world.
5. Oni went from being homeless to being a king in less than one (*weak, week*).

EXERCISE B Proofreading Paragraphs

The following paragraphs contain errors in spelling. Circle the errors, and write the corrections in the space above. The first error has been corrected for you as an example. You should find five more.

weak

Nobody wants to be week. However, being strong can be a disadvantage, as Oni, the main character in this story, finds out. Oni is born with a pair of boots on his feet. Their not plain boots, as anyone might suppose; there magic boots. They make Oni invincible. Yet, when the villagers hear about Oni's power, they are not pleased. Instead, they say to each other, "We don't want him here."

The villagers start to pester Oni and make it plane that they don't want him. Oni no longer can find peace in his home. He must leave.

He travels threw strange country until he finally reaches a town. Oni is shone into a house where he can spend the night. He soon discovers that this town is unusual. For some time, a large eagle has been terrifying the people at night, so they can go outside only when the sun rises. Oni can hear the sound of the great bird coming through the roof of the house. This town needs help, and Oni is just the man for the job!

Copyright © by Holt, Rinehart and Winston. All rights reserved.

NAME ______________________ CLASS ______________ DATE __________

LANGUAGE LINK

Master Frog

retold by Lynette Dyer Vuong **Pupil's Edition page 648**

Style: Using Specific Words

ALEX: What is "Master Frog" about?

ANGELA: "Master Frog" is a good story about a nice frog who becomes a prince.

JULIA: "Master Frog" is an entertaining folk tale about an affectionate frog who changes into a prince.

Whose description of "Master Frog" is more specific? Julia describes the story by using more specific nouns, adjectives, and verbs than Angela. Specific words enable a reader to gain a better understanding of what "Master Frog" is all about. They can also make sentences more fun to write and to read. The sentences below demonstrate how specific nouns, adjectives, and verbs can be used to make general sentences more interesting.

GENERAL: The frog likes a nice girl.

SPECIFIC: The frog adores a devoted princess.

GENERAL: The frog moved closer to the king's pretty chair.

SPECIFIC: The frog hopped closer to the king's luxurious throne.

The chart below shows how nouns, adjectives, and verbs in the examples above became more specific.

Part of Speech	General	Specific
nouns	story girl chair	folk tale princess throne
adjectives	good nice nice pretty	entertaining affectionate devoted luxurious
verbs	becomes likes moved	changes adores hopped

EXERCISE A **Rewriting Sentences**

Rewrite the following sentences and replace the italicized words with more specific ones. (Feel free to change other words in the sentences, too!)

EXAMPLE: Master Frog *went* into the palace to meet the king.

Master Frog bounced into the palace to meet the king.

1. The townspeople liked to *talk* about Giang Dung's marriage. ______________________

____

Copyright © by Holt, Rinehart and Winston. All rights reserved.

2. She decided that Master Frog was a very *good* son. ______________________

3. *Some animals* responded to his mighty roar. ______________________

4. There were animals *entering* the hall from all directions. ______________________

5. The king's older daughters refused to marry a *small* frog. ______________________

6. Kien Tien agreed to marry the frog after his *speech*. ______________________

7. In time, the husband and wife *became* good companions. ______________________

8. Kien Tien was *sad* when she saw her husband's skin on his pillow. ______________________

9. The sisters *made a plan* to find husbands of their own. ______________________

10. The king praised his son-in-law for his *good character traits*. ______________________

EXERCISE B Proofreading a Paragraph

Revise the following paragraph by making words in it more specific. Cross out the word or words that you are going to replace, and write the replacement word or words in the space above. One example has been done for you. Find ten more.

selfish

Nobody knew for sure what became of Kim Chau and Bich Ngoc, the ~~mean~~ older sisters of Kien Tien. Some said that they had gone to live in the hills far from Master Frog's house. They tried to get animals and turn them into people, for they were so unwilling to work that they needed to find good husbands. One day, they tried to catch a lion to see if he might be a strong king in disguise. He didn't like being bothered by these unpleasant women. No one was there to see it, but it was said that the animal ate them.

Copyright © by Holt, Rinehart and Winston. All rights reserved.

NAME ______________________ CLASS ______________ DATE ______________

LANGUAGE LINK

Sealskin, Soulskin

retold by Clarissa Pinkola Estés **Pupil's Edition page 661**

Style: Oral Storytelling

Slowly, cautiously, the old man's boat drew closer to the wonderful creatures.

Read the sentence above to yourself. How would you read it differently if you were speaking this sentence out loud? How would you emphasize the ideas of the sentence? What punctuation clues would you use to show your speaking style? You would probably speak the words *slowly* and *cautiously* very slowly, and you would probably pause at the commas.

Follow these three steps to turn a written manuscript into a powerful oral reading:

1. Read the manuscript carefully; watch for punctuation clues.
2. Think about which oral reading techniques will best interpret those clues.
3. Mark the manuscript with reminders that will help you to remember those techniques.

The following chart identifies some punctuation clues and the techniques and marks that go with them:

Punctuation and Other Clues to Watch For	Techniques for Oral Reading	Marks to Prepare a Manuscript for Oral Reading
commas (,), semicolons (;), colons (:), dashes (—), and periods (.)	Use pauses of varying lengths.	Use a slash (/) to indicate short pauses; use a double slash (//) for longer pauses.
(words in parentheses)	Pause and lower volume.	Mark parentheses or highlight in color.
italicized or underlined words	Use louder volume, with stress placed on the words for emphasis.	Highlight italicized or underlined words.
"words inside quotation marks"	Use a variety of changes in voice, such as changes in volume, quality, rate, and use of accents.	Underline, mark pauses, or use colored highlights to indicate treatment of different characters.
question marks?	Use a rising inflection.	Mark an arrow pointing up and to the right. ↗
exclamation points!	Use a swift change in volume or inflection.	Mark an arrow pointing straight up. ↑
meaningful groups of words	Emphasize meaning by using changes in voice quality, volume, or rate.	Mark a specific word group, underline for emphasis, or use colored highlights.

Copyright © by Holt, Rinehart and Winston. All rights reserved.

NAME ______________________ CLASS ______________ DATE ____________

EXERCISE A Interpreting Clues

The following passages from "Sealskin, Soulskin" have been marked for oral reading. On the lines below each passage, describe how you would read the sentence, based on these marks.

EXAMPLE: "She scooped up the child,/tucked him under her arm,/and half ran and half stumbled toward the roaring sea." emphasize "scooped," pause after "child," emphasize "tucked," pause after "arm," emphasize "ran" and "stumbled"

1. "Well,/he was a lonely man,/ with no human friends but in memory—//and he stayed and watched." ______________________

2. "He could hear the magnificent women laughing . . .//at least they seemed to laugh,/or was it the water laughing at the edge of the rock?"↗ ______________________

3. "Why,//they were putting on their sealskins,/and one by one the seal women were slipping into the sea,/yelping and crying happily." ______________________

4. "A strange wind . . .// It seemed to call to him,/'Oooruk, Ooorukkkk.'" ______________________

5. "'And the boy?'↗/asked the old seal.//'My grandchild?'↗" ______________________

EXERCISE B Marking Sentences with Oral Reading Symbols

The following five passages are from "Sealskin, Soulskin." Read them carefully and watch for punctuation clues that are important for oral readings. Then, mark the passages with notes that would help you remember these clues.

EXAMPLE: "I hurt a human . . .// a man who gave his all to have me//. . . but I cannot return to him, for I shall be a prisoner if I do."

1. "Here, nothing thrives for the asking. The winds blow hard so the people have come to wear their parkas and *mamleks,* boots, sideways on purpose now."
2. "He stepped from the rock, appealing to her, 'Woman . . . be . . . my wife.'"
3. "'I want what I am made of returned to me,' cried the seal woman."
4. "And at once you could tell she wanted to stay with her child, she *wanted* to, but something called her, something older than she, older than he, older than time."
5. "And Ooruk, because it was not his time, stayed."

From "Sealskin, Soulskin" from *Women Who Run With the Wolves* by Clarissa Pinkola Estés, Ph.D. Copyright © 1992, 1995 by Clarissa Pinkola Estés, Ph.D. All performance, derivative, adaptation, musical, audio and recording, illustrative, theatrical, film, pictorial, electronic, and all other rights reserved. Reprinted by permission of ***Dr. Clarissa Pinkola Estés and Ballantine Books, a division of Random House, Inc.***

Copyright © by Holt, Rinehart and Winston. All rights reserved.

Collection One: Out Here on My Own

Rikki-tikki-tavi, page 1

Exercise A

(Vivid verbs double-underlined may vary.)

"One day, a high summer flood washed him out of the burrow where he lived with his father and mother and carried him . . . down a roadside ditch. He found a little wisp of grass . . . there and clung to it till he lost his senses. When he revived, he was lying in the hot sun in the middle of a garden path, very draggled indeed, and a small boy was saying: 'Here's a dead mongoose. Let's have a funeral.'"

Exercise B

(Sentences will vary. Sample responses follow.)

1. The trees swayed gently in the summer breeze.
2. A snake will usually coil before it strikes.
3. I love to see my colt trot happily around the arena.
4. The cat sprang to her feet when the dog charged into the room.
5. When I come home late, I try to creep into the house quietly.
6. During the rainstorm, the children sobbed because they weren't allowed outside.
7. Birds shrieked all around us as we ran through the wooded area where their nests were.
8. The baby bird's wings fluttered as it tried to fly for the first time.
9. Dave was impressed when he saw his younger sister crush the can with one hand.
10. The mother bird was clucking at her babies as they left the nest for the first time.

Song of the Trees, page 3

Exercise A

1. share
2. C
3. has
4. C
5. C
6. feel
7. sits
8. C
9. attack
10. C *or* hopes

Exercise B

A tree, and a tree, and another tree *make* up my secret place. I come here when my duties or a brother *drives* me crazy. *Come,* Papa, soon, for the men and the truck *have* come to take my friends away. As each minute of every hour *goes* by, I grow more worried.

Exercise C

(Sentences will vary. Sample responses follow.)

1. Mama, with the help of Cassie and her brothers, *tries to stop Mr. Andersen.* (singular verb)
2. Not one of David Logan's children *wants to see the trees cut down.* (singular verb)
3. The Logans must decide whether the trees or the money *is more important.* (singular verb)
4. Neither Cassie nor her brothers *like Mr. Andersen.* (plural verb)
5. While David Logan holds the plunger, the group of men *watch nervously.* (plural verb) *or* While David Logan holds the plunger, the group of men *draws closer together.* (singular verb)

The Smallest Dragonboy, page 5

Exercise A

1. attends
2. wanted
3. was
4. makes
5. were
6. falls
7. flew
8. has
9. happens
10. put

Exercise B

1. touches, guards
2. choose, hatch
3. works, hopes
4. breaks, pushes
5. struggles, overcomes

Exercise C

When Mrs. Sanchez *asked* her class what they *thought* about "The Smallest Dragonboy," the students *responded* in various ways.

"It *made* me want to live in Pern!" exclaimed Adam.

"I *did* not like the idea of living in caves," commented Lida.

"I *knew* Keevan would be chosen when Mende *told* him what qualities the dragons *looked* for in a boy."

Copyright © by Holt, Rinehart and Winston. All rights reserved.

Exercise D

(Corrections are shown in italics.)

Keevan is eager to become a dragonboy, but when he is a candidate he *is teased* because of his small size. Beterli, an older boy, especially teases him about being small and *thinks* Keevan shouldn't be allowed to be a candidate. That is why it becomes so important for Keevan to Impress a dragon—he wants to prove himself. There is talk one night at dinner that the younger candidates *might be disqualified* because of the large ratio of dragonboys to eggs, so Keevan believes Beterli when he suggests that Keevan is disqualified from the Impression. In a scuffle afterward, Keevan falls and *breaks* his leg. While he is in his bed recovering, the hatching begins. He *decides* to go to the hatching in spite of his broken leg. Once he gets there, however, he feels embarrassed and tries to hide. So no one is more surprised than Keevan himself when he Impresses the bronze dragon!

Three Skeleton Key, page 7

Exercise A

I *laid* down the book I was reading. I had been *sitting* in the lantern room for hours. It was still too early for the sun to *rise*, but the moonlight reflected brightly on the rocks outside the glass. I knew I should wake my partner and go *lie* down, if only for an hour or two. And yet I *sat* there, my eyes closing, though I tried to stay awake.

A moment later, still struggling with sleep, I heard a strange sound. My eyes popped open! Three skeletal figures *set* down one bony foot after another on the sea-drenched rocks. As they danced, they *laid* their skinless fingers on their naked ribs. Clack, clack, clickity clack! Frightened, I *rose* from my seat. "Oh, no! Not again," I thought. "Not here!"

"*Lie* down, Le Gleo," came a voice in the dark room. "You are dreaming." I *raised* my eyes to the barred window of the asylum. Outside, the moon was full over the French countryside.

Exercise B

1. C
2. sit
3. C
4. C
5. C
6. raise
7. laid
8. C
9. C
10. rise

A Day's Wait, page 9

Exercise A

1. I
2. R
3. I
4. I
5. I

Exercise B

1. got or gotten
2. stole
3. rung
4. spoken
5. wore

Exercise C

(Corrections are shown in italics.)

Having eaten the warm food *made* Schatz feel a little better. He *felt* more alive as soon as he *bit* into the cooked quail. Papa *knew* that Schatz might be lonely if he *took* a walk that afternoon, but he *went* anyway. Papa *stood* near the lake and *threw* a stick for the dog. On the way home, he *shot* two birds for dinner. Schatz's face brightened when Papa *brought* him the wonderful meal.

Collection Two: Who Am I?

from *Homesick,* page 11

Exercise A

(Explanations of word differences will vary. Sample responses follow.)

1. **cramped:** *Cramped* means "crowded and uncomfortable," while *narrow* is simply a descriptive word with no positive or negative connotation.
2. **imposing:** If something is imposing, it is usually scary or forbidding. Something grand is fine, wonderful, or lavish.
3. **grunted:** If someone grunts, he or she is generally uncommunicative. Someone murmuring is speaking in a soft voice.
4. **drooped:** If something droops, it is lifeless. Something that dangles hangs loosely, in such a way that it can swing freely.
5. **stubborn:** *Stubborn* suggests a lack of cooperation. *Determined* has the connotation of being firmly decided.
6. **timid:** If someone is timid he or she is nervous and scared, while someone who is careful is simply taking care.
7. **arrogant:** An arrogant person is proud in an exaggerated and overbearing way.

Copyright © by Holt, Rinehart and Winston. All rights reserved.

8. **distressed:** A distressed person is upset and confused. A person who is puzzled is uncertain about something.

Exercise B

(Responses will vary. Possible responses follow.)

1. tapping
2. asked
3. leaned *or* relaxed
4. took
5. stared *or* gazed

Exercise C

(Responses will vary. Possible responses follow.)

1. The Yangtze River was dark and mysterious.
2. The British school taught the children discipline.
3. Ian Forbes was a very strong-willed boy.
4. The Bund was big and frightening.
5. The Chinese junk was bare and empty.

from *Barrio Boy,* page 13

Exercise A

1. more interesting
2. more
3. more nervous
4. best
5. farther
6. more difficult
7. better
8. most understanding
9. more
10. more educational

Exercise B

(Corrections are shown in italics.)

When Ernesto first met Miss Ryan, he thought she was the *tallest* woman he had ever seen. Although he was frightened by her at first, he soon decided that she was *nicer* than any other teacher at the school. He felt as if she were *prouder* of him than she was of anyone else. Miss Ryan was happy when any student read a new sentence, but Ernesto thought she was *happiest* when he read his sentence. While he always worked hard at school, he worked even *harder* when she was helping him.

Fish Cheeks, page 15

Exercise A

(Adjectives that students should underline in sentences are indicated below.)

1. young, sensitive, impressionable
2. only, Chinese, uncomfortable
3. narrow, American
4. slimy, pale, raw
5. unsophisticated
6. pudding-soft, flattened, cooked, favorite
7. reddened
8. polite, courteous
9. beige, tweed, right
10. older, wiser, better

Exercise B

(Responses will vary. Possible responses follow.)

1. POSITIVE: beautiful, wonderful-smelling, delicious, steaming
   NEGATIVE: disgusting, appalling, leftover, cold
2. POSITIVE: loving, generous, kind, happy, good-hearted
   NEGATIVE: frowning, strange, unfriendly, sour
3. POSITIVE: cozy, warm, cheery, sparkling, clean, spacious
   NEGATIVE: tiny, dingy, dirty, stuffy, smoky, crowded
4. POSITIVE: successful, peaceful, proud, talkative
   NEGATIVE: stingy, loud, obnoxious
5. POSITIVE: new, favorite, most comfortable, prettiest
   NEGATIVE: old, filthy, rumpled, outdated, torn
6. POSITIVE: splendid, great, incredible, anticipated
   NEGATIVE: torturous, dreaded, nightmarish, boring
7. POSITIVE: athletic, dream-filled, carefree, productive
   NEGATIVE: wasted, hopeless, lost, painful

Names/Nombres, page 17

Exercise A

1. DM
2. Referring to Shakespeare as my friend, my mother quoted, "A rose by any other name would smell as sweet."
3. DM
4. DM
5. DM
6. Suddenly interested in ethnicity, people in the 1960s began trying to pronounce foreign names correctly.
7. Wondering if it would ever end, friends listened in amazement to my entire name.
8. DM
9. Reaping the benefits of a large family, I received one gift after another at my graduation party.
10. DM

Exercise B

(Responses will vary. Sample responses follow.)

1. Although I tried hard to say it the way Julia did, the word still sounded different coming out of me.
   or
   Trying hard to say it the way Julia did, I still made the word sound different.
2. As I blushed at all the attention, the other women wanted to know the baby's name.
   or
   Blushing at all the attention, I heard the other women asking me the baby's name.
3. Feeling embarrassed by his own accent, he let his name become more and more Americanized.

ANSWER KEY

Copyright © by Holt, Rinehart and Winston. All rights reserved.

or

Because he felt embarrassed by his own accent, he let his name become more and more Americanized.

4. Questions about her native culture no longer bothered her, as she found her classmates interested in what she told them.

or

Finding her classmates interested in what she told them, she no longer minded their questions about her native culture.

5. Convinced that her friends really liked her, she felt the nicknames they gave her were a sign of their affection.

or

Since she was convinced that her friends really liked her, the nicknames they gave her were taken as a sign of their affection.

The Naming of Names, page 19

Exercise A

_____ 1. The newcomers who arrived from Earth headed for the settlement.

_____ 2. Not understanding Harry's fear, Cora tried to calm him.

M 3. The peach tree grew a new type of blossom that they brought with them.

M 4. Glowing green in the east, Harry noticed the star.

_____ 5. They wondered if the Martians who had lived there first were still in the hills.

M 6. The wind had an effect on the Earth people that blew into the valley.

M 7. Made of blue marble, they moved into the Martian ruins.

M 8. Bathed with mist, the lieutenant gazed at the blue hills.

Exercise B

1. With no way to get home, Harry began to panic.
2. One of the first signs of change was seen in the eyes of the people.
3. The blue marble in the villa was as cool as ice.
4. Everyone in the settlement moved to the hills during the summer.
5. The men from the rocket expected the settlers to be excited to see them.

Exercise C

(Sentences will vary. Sample responses follow.)

1. Harry would not eat the food *that was grown on Mars.*
2. The other men *in the settlement* sat and watched Harry work.
3. The earth houses *that were made out of wood* flaked and peeled in the Martian summer.
4. They explored the marble villas *on the mountain*.
5. *Finally having calmed his fears,* even Harry grew to like life on Mars.

Collection Three: Do the Right Thing

After Twenty Years, page 21

Exercise A

1. Do you have the impression that Jimmy likes his job? Do you think he is envious of Bob's money?
2. What do you think Jimmy was thinking as he walked away from Bob? That night must have been a disappointment for him. (*or* !)
3. How do you think Bob feels about Jimmy? He must be surprised that Jimmy turned him in. (*or* !)
4. Bob probably wishes he had missed his appointment with Jimmy. (*or* !) Do you think Jimmy is glad he kept the date, or not?
5. What a shock! Jimmy and Bob ended up on opposite sides of the law. (*or* !)

Exercise B

(Corrections are shown in boldface.)

Can you imagine how Bob must have felt when he read Jimmy's note? He must have felt as if he had been betrayed by his old friend**.** **(*or* !)** The story tells us that Bob's hand began to shake when he read the note. Why did his hand shake**?** Was he angry**?** Maybe he was embarrassed that Jimmy knew the truth about him**.** After all, he had led a life of crime while Jimmy had remained honest.

And what about Jimmy**?** Was he happy that a criminal was in jail**?** Was he sad that his old friend had ruined his life**?** How do you think Jimmy felt when Bob suggested that Jimmy had always been a bit dull**?** He probably didn't get too angry at Bob**.** Jimmy may not have made a fortune, but at least he had led an honest life. Bob bragged that he had made his fortune by his wits, but his "dull" friend had outwitted him this night**.** (***or* !**)

A Mason-Dixon Memory, page 23

Exercise A

1. The story portrays Dondré as a soft-spoken**,** friendly**,** likable person.
2. ✔

Copyright © by Holt, Rinehart and Winston. All rights reserved.

3. The seniors listened to their coach, looked at one another, and walked off the golf course.
4. Dondré ended his story, tears came to his eyes, and the audience applauded.
5. Clifton Davis is a writer, songwriter, singer, and actor.
6. ✔
7. He noticed Lincoln's tired, unsmiling face.
8. ✔
9. Clifton was young, ambitious, and outgoing.
10. Dondré's friends were loving, courageous, and fair-minded.

Exercise B

(Corrections are shown in boldface.)

Both Dondré and Clifton feel the pain, anger, and frustration of being targets of discrimination. However, both have caring, honorable friends who stand by them. Also, both young African American [omit comma] men put racism behind them, go on with their lives, and achieve success. Dondré speaks as the guest of honor at a banquet, expresses his gratitude to his teammates, and receives a standing ovation. Clifton's loyal boyhood friends make him proud and grateful. His confidence, ambition, and success may be, in part, a gift from them.

The No-Guitar Blues, page 25

Exercise A

1. I
2. I
3. C
4. I
5. I

Exercise B

(Responses will vary. Possible responses follow.)

1. Fausto knows his family is not rich, but that doesn't stop him from asking for a guitar.
2. Programs like *American Bandstand* inspire as well as entertain. Many viewers imitate dancers and musicians they see on TV.
3. You shouldn't expect others to solve your problems for you. Find a way to do it for yourself.
4. C
5. After looking for work for three hours, Fausto is discouraged, but he does not go home.
6. The dog presents a chance to make some money, so Fausto looks for the dog's home.
7. C
8. The collection basket comes to Fausto, and he puts his twenty into the basket.
9. Does Fausto really fool Roger's owners? After all, they seem anxious to help him.
10. Fausto and his grandfather may not like the same music, but Grandpa enjoys teaching him to play the guitarron.

Bargain, page 27

Exercise A

1. Al worked in Mr. Baumer's store.
2. There were two horses tied to Hirsch Brothers' rack.
3. Slade's bill totaled twenty-one dollars and fifty cents.
4. Mr. Baumer saw Slade in front of the saloon's door.
5. The two clerks' shifts always increased before Christmas.

Exercise B

1. Mr. Baumer doesn't want to forget about Slade's bill.
2. If you let the freighters get away with stealing whiskey, they'll do it every time.
3. I'm able to work a few extra days if you need me to.
4. I'd talk to the sheriff about Slade if I were you.
5. There's only one way to stop Slade.

Amigo Brothers, page 29

Exercise A

1. I—"You know, Felix," said Antonio, "maybe we're making too big a deal out of this."
2. I—"What do you mean?" he responded. "I never wanted to fight you!"
3. I—"I mean," said Antonio, "it would be a shame to force my best friend into a losing position."
4. C
5. C

Exercise B

(Corrections are shown in boldface.)

1. "Felix has got a dynamite punch," said Mr. Sayer. "My money's on him."
2. His friend thought about that for a moment. "Yes," he said, "but have you seen Tony move?"
3. "These guys are amigo brothers, though!" observed another man in the crowd. "I heard one of them tell the other that he didn't really want to fight."
4. Mr. Sayer's face reddened. "These boys are cheverote fighters. It will be a fair fight."
5. The man certainly hadn't meant to imply a fixed fight when he said, "These guys are amigo brothers"! (**or** brothers!")

Exercise C

(Sentences will vary. Sample responses follow.)

1. "I'll be staying with my aunt Lucy," Felix told Antonio.
2. "Felix, do you feel the same way I do about the fight?" asked Antonio.

ANSWER KEY

Copyright © by Holt, Rinehart and Winston. All rights reserved.

3. "After seeing the movie," said Felix, "I'm really psyched up for the fight!"
4. Feeling lonely already, he shook Tony's hand and said, "Goodbye."
5. "Give me a quick knockout so that I won't hurt Felix too much," Antonio prayed.

Collection Four: We Rookies Have to Stick Together

Brian's Song, page 31

Exercise A

(Corrections are shown in boldface.)

1. Brian begins to lose weight and to cough**;** as a result**,** he goes into the hospital.
2. The fake draw, screen right**,** for example**,** is a football play that the Bears used.
3. Dick Butkus was a linebacker for Chicago**;** furthermore**,** he was a *big* linebacker!
4. Brian was caught talking**;** consequently**,** he had to sing a fight song in front of everyone.
5. Brian needed his rest**;** therefore**,** the nurse told Gale to leave.

Exercise B

(Responses will vary. Possible responses follow.)

1. Coach Halas noticed Brian's improvement. As a result, he made Brian the number one fullback.

   or

   Coach Halas noticed Brian's improvement; as a result, he made Brian the number one fullback.
2. Gale Sayers and Brian Piccolo roomed together. However, they didn't let the difference in the color of their skin bother them.

   or

   Gale Sayers and Brian Piccolo roomed together; however, they didn't let the difference in the color of their skin bother them.
3. In one game, Brian carried the ball fourteen times for 105 yards. Consequently, he was awarded the game ball.

   or

   In one game, Brian carried the ball fourteen times for 105 yards; consequently, he was awarded the game ball.
4. Football can be a dangerous sport. For example, a quarterback might injure his throwing arm.

   or

   Football can be a dangerous sport; for example, a quarterback might injure his throwing arm.
5. Brian had one operation. Then, he had to undergo another one.

   or

   Brian had one operation, and then he had to undergo another one.

Collection Five: Living in the Heart

User Friendly, page 33

Exercise A

1.	me	**6.**	she
2.	her	**7.**	them
3.	him	**8.**	they
4.	me	**9.**	we
5.	he	**10.**	us

Exercise B

1. C
2. Will Ginny sit between Linda and me?
3. Ginny's family and he had several upsetting surprises.
4. Why did Louis wish to harm Chuck and her?
5. Perhaps the engineers or they will find a bug in the program.

Copyright © by Holt, Rinehart and Winston. All rights reserved.

Miss Awful, page 35

Exercise A

1. Some of Roger's classmates used *coarse* language to describe Miss Orville.
2. The eviction notice was written on official city *stationery*.
3. Some of the parents wanted to complain to the *principal*.
4. Miss Orville asked a volunteer to name the *capital* city of the United States.
5. The school *counselor* and Miss Orville were talking in the hallway.
6. The city councilor was sympathetic but could not prevent the eviction.
7. Roger applied the *brake* and brought his bicycle to a halt.
8. Bending forward at the *waist,* the dance partners bowed to each other.
9. Form a *stationary* line, and do not move until I tell you.
10. The students destroyed the plant, but they did not *break* the pot.

Exercise B

(Corrections are shown in italics.)

I have a fundamental *principle* that guides my teaching. Education is too valuable a treasure to *waste.* We should enjoy learning, of *course*. Write an educational goal on the official school *stationery* that I give you. If you need *counsel,* I will be happy to advise you. We will not take a *break* until everyone has finished.

The Only Girl in the World for Me, page 37

Exercise A

(Sentences will vary. Sample responses follow.)

1. Was Bill jealous of Sidney while Sidney was going out with the goddess?
2. Before Bill left his seat, he thought of Romeo.
3. Probably because people were curious, they looked at Bill and the girl.
4. Bill's heart was consumed with conquest when Cupid's arrow struck it.
5. Cosby alludes to Mercury, who is the Roman god of messages.

Exercise B

(Sentences will vary. Sample responses follow.)

1. The first paragraph gives Cosby's age as twelve.
2. Western Union sends telegrams.
3. Apparently, sixth-graders write notes, not make conversation.
4. At the beginning of *Love and Marriage* is a dedication to Camille.
5. *Romeo and Juliet* is appealing because the story dramatizes the fates of two young lovers.

Collection Six: This Old Earth

Sky Woman, page 39

Exercise A

1. "Accidents will happen—it wasn't my fault!" said Sky Woman's daughter.
2. "You'll live to regret this," said the chief as Sky Woman fell from Sky World.
3. Sky Woman's warnings to her daughter went in one ear and out the other.
4. "The nice things Flint does," said the Good Mind, "are few and far between. Getting him to say 'thank you' is harder than climbing Mount Everest in a single day."
5. Flint scowled. "Well, at least I do whatever I want to—not like the Good Mind, who's so good he bores me to tears."

Exercise B

(Sentences will vary. Sample responses follow.)

1. People in Sky World used to be *as happy and as carefree as children.*
2. Things would have turned out much differently if the chief of Sky World had *re-examined his actions.*
3. Uprooting the Sky Tree made a hole *as big as a city* in Sky Land.
4. Sky Woman's daughter *shot up like mercury in a thermometer.*
5. Getting rid of Flint was *harder than keeping cool in August.*

Exercise C

(Revisions will vary. Possible revisions are shown in italics.)

When Sky Woman fell through the hole in Sky Land, *she didn't know what to do*. Luckily, however, the animals decided to *help her out.* They dredged up earth from the bottom of the sea, and Sky Woman used the land that grew out of it to plant seeds from the Sky Tree. Pretty soon, trees and plants were growing *like a thick carpet* all over the new continent.

Copyright © by Holt, Rinehart and Winston. All rights reserved.

When she saw the way the animals had helped her, Sky Woman thought she might be able to be happy again. But with the birth of her grandsons, her troubles began afresh. One of her grandsons, the Good Mind, was *well-behaved,* but Flint *did anything he could to get into trouble.* He did everything he could to destroy all of the hard work that Sky Woman and the Good Mind had put into making their new home a pleasant place to live.

When the Earth Shakes, page 41

Exercise A

1. young man
2. ashamed
3. terrified
4. positively
5. tease

Exercise B

(Sentences will vary. Sample responses follow.)

1. Notice how that mountain has split apart.
2. Since there was oil sitting on top of the water, the fires on shore took off across the sea.
3. The waves were huge, and they were coming right at us! The whole waterfront totally vanished!
4. During the earthquake, automobiles were thrown about the street as if they were rubber balls.
5. The tension in the earth released during an earthquake is much like that released by a bow on an arrow.
6. When the earthquake hit, most of the citizens in Turnagain were at home.
7. After the quake, most people saw that their houses were wrecked.

from *Survive the Savage Sea,* page 43

Exercise A

1. P
2. A
3. A
4. P
5. P

Exercise B

1. Dougal's good humor lifted Sandy's spirits.
2. The Robertsons wasted nothing—not even turtle blood.
3. The children understood the situation to be very grave.
4. A lack of rain threatened their water supply.
5. A Japanese fishing crew finally spotted the hand-held flares.

Exercise C

Responses will vary.

Antaeus, page 45

Exercise A

1. D
2. S
3. D
4. S
5. D
6. S
7. D
8. D
9. S
10. S

Exercise B

(Sentences will vary. Sample responses follow.)

1. Don't you have any woods around here?
2. You mean you don't have fields in which to raise anything?
3. In the spring we could raise watermelons, garden vegetables, and anything else we want.
4. Once it's cultivated, you'll have a crop.
5. All of you seem determined to raise grass.
6. I have a quarter. How much do the rest of you have?
7. We were just planning to plant watermelon.
8. They would be wonderful to eat while we lie on the grass.
9. You have no right.
10. Nobody can interfere with anyone else's land.

Collection Seven: Our Classical Heritage

The Origin of the Seasons, page 47

Exercise A

1. P; Hades
2. P; farmers
3. G
4. P; nature
5. G

Exercise B

(Sentences will vary. Sample responses follow.)

1. The parched flowers cried out for rain.
2. His favorite activity is eating.
3. We were awakened by screaming sirens.
4. Complaining won't get you anywhere.
5. We rescued the trapped turtles from the net.
6. Your singing has improved.

Copyright © by Holt, Rinehart and Winston. All rights reserved.

7. Sheila appreciated the teacher's encouraging words.
8. Who left the water running?
9. Wandering through the mall is not my favorite pastime.
10. Please throw out those ruined boxes.

Orpheus, the Great Musician, page 49

Exercise A

1. simile
2. metaphor
3. personification
4. metaphor
5. metaphor
6. personification
7. simile
8. simile
9. personification
10. simile

Exercise B

(Sentences will vary. Sample responses follow.)

Music

Metaphor—Music was his life.

Simile—That music sounds like a sputtering car motor.

Personification—His music smiled down on me and rocked me to sleep.

Underworld

Metaphor—The underworld was a prison to Persephone.

Simile—The underworld was as confining as a prison cell.

Personification—For seven months the underworld held Persephone in its grasp.

Echo and Narcissus, page 51

Exercise A

1. you're
2. It's
3. its
4. who's
5. whose
6. your
7. It's
8. Who's
9. You're
10. its

Exercise B

(Corrections are shown in italics.)

I think it's fun to hear voices echo. You shout your message across a ravine, and *you're* sure to hear part of it return. You hear the sound the first time when the sound waves reach *your* ears by the most direct route. Then, if the sound also hits a large object like a building, *its* waves bounce back, and you hear them a second time. When you hear the sound a second time, *it's* an echo. Even though you know *it's* just sound waves bouncing back, *who's* sure? At night when *your* imagination runs wild and the moon hides *its* face, you might wonder if it's Echo herself *whose* voice calls out, "*Who's* that?"

The Flight of Icarus, page 53

Exercise A

(The modified word is shown in parentheses.)

1. adverb (listened)
2. adjective (father)
3. adjective (feathers)
4. adverb (there)
5. adjective (he)

Exercise B

1. calmly
2. perfectly
3. quickly
4. mournful
5. swift

Exercise C

(Sentences will vary. Sample responses follow.)

1. adjective
   Be careful when you lift heavy objects.
2. adverb
   The man slowly rose from his seat.
3. adverb
   Do you water this plant often?
4. adverb
   Speak quietly in the library.
5. adjective
   The park was filled with happy children.

The Labors of Hercules, page 55

Exercise A

1. good
2. well
3. well
4. good
5. well

Exercise B

1. Diana cared well for her sacred stag.
2. How well have you read this story?
3. C
4. C
5. After a long rest, he felt well again.
6. Eurystheus thought Hercules performed each task a little too well.
7. C
8. Eurystheus wasn't sure if bringing the savage mares to his palace was a good idea.
9. Hippolyte fought well, but she was no match for Hercules.
10. C

ANSWER KEY

Copyright © by Holt, Rinehart and Winston. All rights reserved.

King Midas and the Golden Touch, page 57

Exercise A

1. Echo
2. Persephone
3. Cerberus
4. Hercules
5. Midas

Exercise B

(Sentences will vary. Sample responses follow.)

1. All her investments bring her lots of money.
2. Don't go there, because it's dangerous and scary.
3. You'd have to have fifty brains to figure all these answers at once.
4. He acts like he's better than mere mortals, and that turns people off.
5. From the expression on her face, you'd think she'd just seen a ghost.

Exercise C

(Sentences will vary. Sample responses follow.)

1. He's the David Robinson of our class.
2. That Chihuahua barked at that Goliath of a Great Dane.
3. He has a bank account the size of Donald Trump's.
4. I have a headache the size of the Grand Canyon.
5. She plays the piano like Mozart.
6. She runs as fast as Florence Griffith Joyner.
7. He is as dedicated to his cause as Martin Luther King, Jr., was to the civil rights movement.
8. He is funnier than Jim Carrey.

Aesop's Fables, page 59

Exercise A

1. badly
2. bad
3. badly
4. badly
5. bad
6. bad
7. bad
8. badly
9. bad
10. badly

Exercise B

(Corrections are shown in italics.)

In the fable "The Dog and the Bone," a hungry dog needs a meal very badly. He finally finds an old bone, and though it smells *bad,* he quickly grabs it. He feels *bad* that he can't eat it right away, but another badly starved dog might see him.

Homeward the dog trots until he comes to a *badly* swollen stream. The dog looks into the water and sees his reflection. But with his bad eyesight, he thinks he is seeing another dog.

"That dog has a bone that's better than mine, and I want it *badly*!" thinks our hero. "I'll bark at him and scare him so *badly* that he'll drop the bone and leave it to me."

Of course, when the dog opens his mouth to bark, he loses the bone he already has. "Bad bone day," he mumbles, as he heads home.

Collection Eight: 900 Cinderellas: Our World Heritage in Folklore

Aschenputtel, page 61

Exercise A

1. Aschenputtel's stepsisters ought to have been nicer to her.
2. Her stepmother wouldn't let her go anywhere, not even to the festival.
3. The prince sat by himself until the beautiful girl entered the festival.
4. In her golden gown Aschenputtel looked rather [or somewhat] like a foreign princess.
5. The prince didn't understand why Aschenputtel was running away.

Exercise B

(Responses will vary. Sample responses follow, with the replacement word(s) in italics.)

I used to think that "Cinderella" was just a movie. Now I know that it is a fairy tale that is known nearly *everywhere* in the world. By reading "Aschenputtel," I learned that fairy tales come in *a lot* of different versions. This version of "Cinderella" might *have* been lost if the Brothers Grimm hadn't written it down.

My favorite part of "Aschenputtel" is the ending. The reason I like the end is *that* it shows why it's important to be a good person. The story is pretty violent, but in a fairy tale, that's *all right*. If it were a true story, it could *have* been pretty scary. I guess that's *why* people like fairy tales so much. People *rather* like to hear stories about good and evil, especially when there are happy endings.

The Algonquin Cinderella / Yeh-Shen, page 63

Exercise A

1. already
2. except
3. altogether
4. two
5. effect

Copyright © by Holt, Rinehart and Winston. All rights reserved.

Exercise B

(Corrections are shown in italics.)

Oochigeaskw and the Invisible One were married in the fall, before the cold weather began. The people of the village were *all together* before the lake, *except* for Oochigeaskw's sisters who were *too* ashamed to come to the wedding. They had been quite strongly *affected* by the news of their sister's good fortune. At first they were jealous, but *then* they began to see the error of their ways. The mean older sister was not *altogether* mean, after all. She wished that she had acted differently and wondered *whether* she ought to apologize. But she thought she had been *too* mean to ever be forgiven. Oochigeaskw, however, wished for her sisters *to* attend her wedding. She went to find her sisters, and they were happy to *accept* her kind invitation.

Oni and the Great Bird, page 65

Exercise A

1. piece
2. plane
3. their
4. shown
5. week

Exercise B

Nobody wants to be (week) [weak]. However, being strong can be a disadvantage, as Oni, the main character in this story, finds out. Oni is born with a pair of boots on his feet. (Their) [They're] not plain boots, as anyone might suppose; (there) [they're] magic boots. They make Oni invincible. Yet, when the villagers hear about Oni's power, they are not pleased. Instead, they say to each other, "We don't want him here."

The villagers start to pester Oni and make it (plane) [plain] that they don't want him. Oni no longer can find peace in his home. He must leave.

He travels (threw) [through] strange country until he finally reaches a town. Oni is (shone) [shown] into a house where he can spend the night. He soon discovers that this town is unusual. For some time, a large eagle has been terrifying the people at night, so they can go outside only when the sun rises. Oni can hear the sound of the great bird coming through the roof of the house. This town needs help, and Oni is just the man for the job!

Master Frog, page 67

Exercise A

(Responses will vary. Sample responses follow, with the replacement word(s) in italics.)

1. The townspeople liked to *gossip* about Giang Dung's marriage.
2. She decided that Master Frog was a very *dutiful* son.
3. *Lions, tigers, and bears* responded to his mighty roar.
4. There were animals *running into* the hall from all directions.
5. The king's older daughters refused to marry a *tiny* frog.
6. Kien Tien agreed to marry the frog after his *threatening croak*.
7. In time, the husband and wife *grew to be* good companions.
8. Kien Tien was *devastated* when she saw her husband's skin on his pillow.
9. The sisters *plotted* to find husbands of their own.
10. The king praised his son-in-law for his *intelligence and good manners*.

Exercise B

(Responses will vary. Sample responses follow, with the replacement word(s) in italics.)

Nobody knew for sure what became of Kim Chau and Bich Ngoc, the selfish older sisters of Kien Tien. Some said that *the sisters* had gone to live in the hills far from Master Frog's *palace*. They tried to get animals and *transform* them into people, for they were so *lazy* that they needed to find *rich* husbands. One day, they tried to *capture* a lion to see if he might be a *powerful* king in disguise. He didn't like being bothered by these *annoying* women. No one was there to *witness their deaths*, but it was said that the *beast devoured* them.

Sealskin, Soulskin, page 69

Exercise A

1. pause after *Well,* pause after *man,* longer pause after *memory*
2. longer pause after *laughing,* pause after *laugh,* upward inflection after question mark
3. emphasize *Why,* double pause after *why,* pause after *sealskins,* pause after *sea,* emphasize *yelping and crying*

Copyright © by Holt, Rinehart and Winston. All rights reserved.

4. longer pause after *wind,* pause after *him,* use different voice for *"Oooruk, Ooorukkkk"*
5. different voice for quotations, pause after *boy,* upward inflection after question marks, double pause after *old seal*

Exercise B

(Responses will vary. Sample responses follow.)

1. "Here,/nothing thrives for the asking.//The winds blow hard so the people have come to wear their parkas and *mamleks,*/boots,/sideways on purpose now."
2. "He stepped from the rock,/appealing to her,/'Woman . . . //be . . . //my wife.'"
3. "'I want what I am made of returned to me,'/cried the seal woman."
4. "And at once you could tell she wanted to stay with her child,/she wanted to,/but something called her,/something older than she,/older than he,/older than time."
5. "And Ooruk,/because it was not his time,/stayed."

From "Sealskin, Soulskin" from *Women Who Run With the Wolves* by Clarissa Pinkola Estés, Ph.D. Copyright © 1992, 1995 by Clarissa Pinkola Estés, Ph.D. All performance, derivative, adaptation, musical, audio and recording, illustrative, theatrical, film, pictorial, electronic, and all other rights reserved. Reprinted by permission of ***Dr. Clarissa Pinkola Estés and Ballantine Books, a division of Random House, Inc.***

Copyright © by Holt, Rinehart and Winston. All rights reserved.